Pollen, Salt, & Chimes

Pollen, Salt, & Chimes:

New Poems & Others

By Kurt Heinzelman

PINYON PUBLISHING

Montrose, Colorado

Cover Photograph by Susan Sage Heinzelman

Photograph of Kurt Heinzelman by Eric Beggs

First Edition: December 2024

Pinyon Publishing
23847 V66 Trail, Montrose, CO 81403
www.pinyon-publishing.com

Library of Congress Control Number: 2024947105
ISBN: 978-1-936671-99-1

ACKNOWLEDGMENTS

The poems in this volume that are not new were selected from three volumes published before 2013. The two oldest—*The Halfway Tree* (2000) and *Black Butterflies* (2007)—appeared in very limited letterpress editions, both created by Randolph Bertin. The third, *The Names They Found There* (2011), was from Pecan Grove Press; it was the last volume produced by that important small press in San Antonio, Texas, which ceased operations with the passing of its founding editor, Palmer Hall. These three volumes have been long unavailable. The purpose of the present volume is to unite a selection of these three books, plus a group of new poems, with my last two books from Pinyon Publishing, both still in print: *Intimacies and Other Devices* (2013) and *Whatever You May Say* (2017). My utmost thanks to Pinyon for the ongoing support of Susan Elliott Entsminger and the late Gary Entsminger.

I also wish to thank the editors of various journals in the U.S. and the U.K. who first published some of the poems in the present volume:

Arion; Balcones Review; Blue Mesa Review; Borderlands; Desire: A Harry Ransom Center Exhibition Catalogue; The Dirty Goat; Ekphrasis: A Poetry Journal; Georgia Review; Inventory; Marlboro Review; Massachusetts Review; New Edinburgh Review (Scotland); *Notre Dame Review; Poetry; Poetry Northwest; Southwest Review; Tar River Review; Texas Observer; Texas Poetry Calendar; Translation;* and *Utter: The Journal*

And to the editors of collections where some of these poems have been reprinted:

Big Sky, Big Hair: Best of the Texas Poetry Calendar; Borestone Mountain Poetry Awards Anthology; Literary Austin; Odes and Elegies: Eco-Poetry from the Texas Gulf Coast; The Weight of Addition: An Anthology of Texas Poetry

This book is dedicated to:

Ryker, Fleur, Arwyn, Soleil, and *Waverly*

And to the memory of the great-grandparents they never knew:

Frank William Heinzelman (1907-1997)
Katherine Kundert Heinzelman (1910-1992)

—dairy farmers of Swiss and German ancestry whose lives spanned virtually the entire twentieth century and whose families farmed their small corners of the American prairie in the old ways.

Contents

—SELECTED POEMS—

Sunrise Without Trees   3
Condos in Cornfields   6
On Wisconsin   8
Mother's Funeral   10
Local Stone   12
Ode to a Toaster   14
Where Do You Come From?   17
Fall Clearing   28
Something to Call It   30
Bumping Whales   31
Divorce Triptych   33
Her Childhood   38
Broken Things   39
The Halfway Tree   41
The Marfa Lights   44
The Origin of Circles   46
Summoning Dolphins   48
First Assignment   50
Pedagogy   52

The Old School   54

A Valediction: In Memory of the Birthday Party for St.
    Ignatius   57

Unaccompanied Instrument   63

Study for the Figure of Time   65

Post-Conquest   66

The Thousand Fragments   67

Le Tombeau de Paul Celan   70

Jacobus Vrel   73

The Art of Somnambulism   75

Assignment: Drawing Water   77

Pine   78

Peonies   80

Evening   81

Onion Milk   82

Bifocals   83

Midday, Midsummer   85

Daughters of Proteus   86

Sister Noire   88

Vermont   89

Afterwards   91

Ground Wars   94

Like Hershey's for Chocolate   95

Civilities in Time of Civil War   97

Visiting the Somme   98

Cliff Tombs: Pinara   102

Allianoi   104

What We Thought We Came For   107

The Eagle Owls at Crow, A Bird Sanctuary Near
    Ringwood on the Road to the New Forest   109
Near Surfers Paradise   110
Swansea Bay, Old and New   111
The Devil's Rosary   113
North of Austin: 1980   119
The Names They Found There   121
"Pflugerville Faces Sprawl"   123
Way Out West   125
In This Our Neighborhood   126
Fear a Joke Inside   128
Ralph Waldo Emerson Visits the Fenway, 1880   130
Another's Brass   132

—WRITINGS WITH OTHERS—

Texas (Borges)   137
Ronsard's Complaint (Ronsard)   138
To Rimbaud (Verlaine)   139
What Remains (Horace)   140
Ecstasy (Hugo)   142
The Moon Rises (Lorca)   143
The Sun (Baudelaire)   144
Mote (Ungaretti)   145
Early One Morning (Heine)   147

Paris, 1856 (Borges)   148

Camden, 1892 (Borges)   149

These Wings (Horace)   150

Ballade of Sayings From the Days of Yore
    (Queneau)   151

Sidecar Sapphics (Horace)   153

Daphne: An Ode in the Pindaric Style (Ovid and Petah
    Coyne)   154

—NEW POEMS—

1

February. Elev. 233'   163

The Answer   164

The Granddaughter Dresses for the Last Spring
    Game   165

Rain Chances   167

Springtime Dogleg Blues   168

Post-Op   170

Mother's Laundry Was Done in the Cellar   172

Before   173

2

America Goes to War: Green County, Wisconsin, April
    1917   177
American Flight   179
Ode: Pandemic/Invasion   180

3

Changing Time Zones   185
Facing Pages   186
Nocturne in Search of a Key   188
Recharge Zones   190
Skid Marks   191
How Days Break   193
Walking Home After Drinking With Friends   194
The Real Something   196
That Uncertain Something   198
Texas Parable   199
Days of Flying Frijoles   200

4

Musician. Comedian. Muralist   205
    1. The Vocal Line   205
    2. The Stand-Up's Constitutional   206
    3. Across a Crowded Room   208

5

Fences: An Explanation   213
Ground Cover in Flyover Country   217
Precedents   218

Notes   227

About   233

Responses to Previous Works   235

—SELECTED POEMS—

Sunrise Without Trees

Things grow old
so quickly
in the fields.
　　　　　—Richard Jeffries,
　　　　　　Field & Hedgerow

Before long
it will be dawn
in Auroraville, Wisconsin.

Quiet as insects
the mares circle
and spread out

end to end,
a splayed green edge
of sweet corn

banking these
alfalfa fields.
Rising from rye grass

a few still to be
emptied cows traipse
slantwise before the sun.

Past the combine,
the honey wagon
still in shadow,

beyond the sway-backed
winter salt licks,
air assumes

an air of knowing
how long
and since when.

Morning
is an ageless girl,
hands warm with eggs,

and a voiceless
old man bearded
with his own breath

stroking his glass
and rocking
a little harder.

In a world without
trees when the light
comes it stays, pulsing

as leaves would
if there were any
wind. The back

lining the road that led to the woods
laid out now with stakes of wood

some flagged, some numbered,
a few with names.

.

On Wisconsin

A mile off, the two main roads (those with numbers) meet now
at an ALL-WAY STOP, and another rural town is entirely bypassed.
Coming back I had forgotten about how much was marsh,
in late spring how the back acres of our one-room, state-graded
schoolhouse turned riparian, water backing all the way up
to where we played "Robin Hood's Barn" around the barn
perched on a rise or "Prisoner's Base" starting from where
the carousel sits waist-high now in burdock and nettle
but still nearly rust free even yet. When flooding shut down
County Trunk Q, the town itself closed around its one street.

What I remember (from living in coastal arroyos now) was
wind. Up the stairs of our farmhouse was a landing with four
bedrooms off it but without any hallway between. In that landing
where stars fought for space in the skylights was the biggest
bed of all. There I found faces in its burled head- and foot-board.
Come spring, we sat on the screened-in porch that wrapped
three sides of the house and watched clouds bruise the backlit
sky out of which, like little tipped jars of blackberry preserves,
tornadoes dropped, jamming up the horizon But wherever
or if ever they touched down remained largely a mystery.

The fall Sputnik went up was when Outer Space turned Red.
Winds worsened. Our team for now remained the Braves, but
the mayor of our next town wanted to change *its* name from Red
Granite. That winter I wiped my palms wet on cellar walls, though
if summer's mud potholed cornfields, drought-dry tassels

flew off in the wind. On a winter night my father announced
he was four years younger than manned flight. Visitors recalled
how, weekends for the Sylvester Township Cubs, he caught
a pitcher, later VP at First National, who blew his brains out
at the first whisperings of fraud. So many accounts were depleted

nothing that vanished ever materialized anywhere else again.

Mother's Funeral

By the time I got there I hadn't seen her
in sixteen months and she'd been dead
two days. In the open coffin she looked
ten years younger. "Just like herself,"
as more than one person I couldn't
put a name to pointed out too *viva*
voce, watching my reaction closely.
Later, I reached out, touching
the corner of the coffin as it went down,
shivering in the snow of the first day
of spring. Then I spoke to my father
like my father. After that, there came a—
I don't know what you'd call it.
It's what a "wake" is to a people with
a faith not ours. From the cemetery
at the edge of town, just beyond
the last street lights, everybody
drives more or less together back
into town, to a mums-bepetaled,
overheated Legion hall and eats
cheese—some of it yellow, some of it
white, some of it yellow and white—
on triangles of crustless bread
while relatives are closing up the quarter
centuries between visits, some of whom
you genuinely are glad have come.

Back home, over small drinks, we told
our stories, but the one that had me

laughing out loud almost was how much
you would have enjoyed all this, your own
aftermath, the gossip and the company,
the family altogether in one place,
before this unabashed floweriness
stiffs us and death's sole aftermath
becomes us.   Just us. Who eat and talk,
drink what we need to drink.

Local Stone

When I rebuilt the wall
that holds my house up
even yet, my father liked
the local stone so much
he took some home with him
from Texas to where he
lived.   He liked its touch,
the porous sleekness,
grooved as driftwood,
though it was squared
enough to edge a border
of his drive, the limit
of his garden. Four
more years of thaws
and frosts and those soft
southern fieldstones
were dust. At his funeral
last month they fired guns,
real guns, and played a tape
of Taps with too much hiss
for the hickory-lined
corner of that northern
graveyard, the farm
where he was born still
visible on the slope beyond.
They handed me the flag,
folded, off the casket.
They offered a salute.
Driving off, the coffin

still on its scaffold,
above ground, still to be
interred, I saw reflected
in the polished red
Wisconsin granite
myself passing through
the place on the stone
where the date of his
death should have been
but was blank.

Ode to a Toaster

It's not true
Edison
invented you before
the light bulb,
though who knows?—
thermodiffusion,
as from a switched coil,
is less complex
than incandescence
if less
ancient than fire.
You were my first
gift to myself,
costing not less
than twice
what you now do,
and yet
I have lived
without
your apple-cheeked kind
going on
thirty years.
Now
my father is dead
I will say he never
knowingly
told a lie
though he spoke sometimes
of Edison as his

contemporary,
promoting
for thirty years
the Power & Light's
electrification
of rural America
and from time
to time
of you
as the world's first
small appliance.
He kept
after my mother
died
their old GE
4-slicer,
a fire hazard
with its worn cloth
cord taped
all the way down
to its antique
unsealed plug
but which still turned
each slice
a just brown
right to the end
when I gave it to Goodwill
along with his
Reddy

Kill-O-Watt
tie clasp
and matching cuff links,
things which had come to seem
too odd
to go on finding
places for,
as is the way, perhaps,
with radiance
and the things it raises
to the power of air
or light.

Where Do You Come From?

Si me preguntáis de dónde vengo …
—Neruda

Back before I ever lived anywhere
anyone would have called a town,
a place with a traffic light—street
lamps at least, ones that kept going on
well past the point where the only streets
kissed like the two spokes of a crucifix—
I thought looking down roads like those
meant I was seeing past and future both.
I think I know that I was not yet seven.
Streets were what I still called "roads."

*

"Towns," I thought, were where the streets
had numbers. Where there were cross-
streets. More than a few. And numbered, too.

So you could live at 5th and 10th,
pretend your house a dime store
like the Woolworth's down by the river

where all the shops were, though here
the kids who gathered, threw balls, also
went missing. But no one was ever lost.

Was it because not enough important
people died yet that our schools were named
only for the four winds? (Mine was

East School, one of those compass points
on which arithmetic and alphabet
unscrolled across an abacus of streets.)

The towns around us, we were taught,
comprised a proud presidential stew—
Madison, Jefferson, Monroe—but because

no football pride yet stirred, when asked
where we were from, we'd ladle out
a county name, a township's, even.

Or else, because why not, we lied.

*

It was back, that is, when roads
were still roads and not highways,
were dirt or gravel, had names,
if they had names at all,
like Route OP or QE—
key-wrecks on a manual
typewriter you would one day
try to teach yourself
to master, using every finger.

Behind the fields of corn where
no road went were shacks,
a "shantytown" you'd call it now,
to which you never went, never
really even dreamed of going.
Where migrant workers stayed.
"Stayed" is what you heard,
not "lived. "Stayed" is how you
learned what "migrant" meant,
learned it from what people said.

Meanwhile you picked asparagus
on your own, from roadside clutches
before all the roads got paved
and broad-band herbicides
put an end to wayside growing.
You collected morels of your own
in places only locals knew. That's
what you thought that "locals"
were, ones who could cross
or leave a field the way
they entered it, without fear
of buckshot, and find there
things no market ever sold.

Once a month at school you chewed
a goiter tablet: an acrid, anise-y

sweetness—not bad, in fact. But why?
"To Protect Against
Deficiencies of Iodine
Among the Inland Citizenry"
No one had yet thought to add
iodine to salt. And the only margarine
was white. Dyeing oleo yellow
to better resemble butter
was still illegal in
"America's Dairyland."

(Some things can be understood
only after you have lived
that close to sweet corn.)

*

Into this world my mother was hurled
the same day Leo Tolstoy froze to death—
she in a rural Green County bedroom
without heat, he outside the Astapovo station
waiting for a train, like the one bringing
Blaise Cendrars and the twentieth century
from Paris to Siberia. By the clock
it was 8 A.M. Both places. But time
wobbled back then. When the hands
of Julian and Gregorian time

pressed together, days were lost.
Still, it was snowing. Both places.

      At his death Tolstoy was the same age
she would be the year she died,
baptized and confirmed and married
all by the same Wisconsin pastor,
a German-speaking radical evangelical
refugee from Switzerland (as Blaise
was, as her parents were)—her birth,
his death, both coming (though my knowing it
lay fifty years more in coming)
a single month before human nature
changed forever, or so postulated
Virginia's calendar of the new century.

*

The geophysics

where I

come from:

time divides

only as

space is

inhabited

*

Where we lived
when we were
"country," when
we lived on
the land, they'd
plant over
ground on which
outhouses
stood once—fine
plots these were
(they said) for
cucumbers,
but only
those bound for
pickledom.

*

Everyone who counted backed it—
the return to wartime time—
and so Wisconsin buckled:

daylight savings arrived.
Or came back anyway.
But at first it came back
one state only, sometimes
one county only, at a time.
Over in Ohio, a thirty-minute
trip for groceries took you
though four time zones.
And the farmers never really
got on board. Why not? A)
it meant you milked both times
in darkness. B) it smelled of
Commie plots, like adding
fluoride to toothpaste—or,
what's next, drinking water?
C) it meant that schoolchildren
stood in subzero darkness
waiting for their buses to arrive
on new paved roads where cars
were going fast, so fast, so fast
(*don't you know?*) these days …

*

And then we moved to a place
where all the schools had names.
We lived on the far eastside
on a corner lot opposite the new,

the one and only, high school
(it had a football team), built two years
before our house. And that's as
far as our town—okay, city—went.
A steep ridge behind the school
marked the place where the prairie
found itself again, its black glacial
loam continuing to plow many
feet deep, and a hundred miles more,
into Lake Michigan. Summer before
my senior year I worked the crew
that built the streets that went beyond
my school that sent me another
thousand or so miles on.

*

1910: year of my mother's birth,
and 90% of North Americans
were rural. Now only 3%
can be said to "live on the land."
Perhaps that is partly why
half our states suffer sizable
populations of feral hogs,
none more so than Texas.
My buddy Beggsy took me up
to Mustang Ridge, a fossil name
in the onomasticon of Texas
but a place with sound if not sight

range of the new municipal
airport, carved from the bones
of an old SAC base with ICBM
silos underground, once a prime
Cold War target, but now boasting
Aeroméxico's four weekly flights,
the airport's claim to being
"international."

What we were looking for
were ancient submarine volcanic
vents from back when Central
Texas was all a warm and shallow
sea. What we found were convex
at times like mini-ice-age moraines
and at times concave like rootings
made by pigs. Where we found magma,
a rank smell came with it, a rough
thrashing of underbrush a god makes
assuming the body of a beast, treading
some hapless human girl in thrall
to all that wildness, mystery, heat.

*

Going one way past our house
in town the road (or street) dead-

ended in a quarry, flooded long ago,
appropriated as a swimming hole,
and dead-ended also the other way
in a thickly wooded city block
in which a single house stood,
cedar-shaked and widow-walked,
a triple-decker no one would condemn
as long as the widow lived.

(There were the pre-fab
jokes, of course, like
how you would know …)

In due course, of course, down it went.
The city carved a new road through there,
a street whose S-curve X-ed out every ghost
and was "just the thing" to slow through-traffic.
Two A-frames, each with a three-car garage,
went up on either side. A few trees were spared.

*

Where the new Interstate
crossed the two-lane macadam,
a road we called East Avenue,
the plan was to put stop signs
at every on- and off-ramp,

but greater minds, the ones
for whom car lights are like
particles doing the wave
in Einstein's brain, foresaw
these four random corners

of a Middle American inter-
section spiraling outward
galactically and added
two lanes to the macadam
and elevation to the interchange.

That Sunday, the one following
the ribbon cutting, my father
piled all of us into his big-
finned Century for our Sunday
outing, and we drove and drove

up, round, over, and down
that wild, 4-leafed, I-road
cloverleaf, the likes of which
had never come this close to
any of our wild provincial lives.

Fall Clearing

Now as we turn the garden upside down,
now as we pack the rose trees lengthways
in the earth, the razing of the ground
becomes the working in of ground,
and all fall long becomes a sort of spring
when, if we're together, we'll do it all again.

A last run of the mower mulches leaves,
my whistle chipping at the brittle air.

*

Around the white stones of the raised deck,
I break wild runners from the blistered grapes,
revealing the arborvitae's delicate
traceries of green. The flower beds
are steeped in leaves, the patio picked bone-clean.
Pressing down, we've worked the stubble in.

*

I watch geese stroke against the sky
their shadows under them. The sky falls from them,
clear. I look around (you've suddenly gone in)—

then seal exposures, caulk the sills, and kneel
to fit the back stormdoor against its stops.
Inside, we no longer see into each other's breath.

Something to Call It

It is vain for you to rise up early, to sit up late, to eat
the bread of sorrows, for so he giveth his beloved sleep.
—Psalms 127

Let's call it screwing up. My mother called it
"a case of too many irons in the fire"
and I quote. The woman I live with
occasionally refers to it, walking home at night
from a concert, in little Indian pipes of breath.
The sky looks like water grief had walked.

I love her, love my mother, don't I?
And I salute them both. Somewhere
(in Gaelic, I think) there's a word for all this—
the mouth filled with laughter, the tongue
full of song. But it's not a word I'll go
any further into: don't try to make me.

I'm putting on my gimme hat and my FAILED
MARXIST T-shirt under a sweatshirt that says RELAX.
That's just half of it. Here's the other half.
Home for the weekend, like a salesman
whose Osterizer jammed crushing ice
for daiquiris and margaritas a minute

before company shows up, I sometimes
just want to hang it up. See if it melts.
Or rusts. Or what. Sometimes I try sleeping
it off, a bag of mothballs on an empty shelf.
Sometimes I think, "Screw this." Sometimes I just
think, curled up, smoking, well into the night.

Bumping Whales

Campobello Island
Bay of Fundy
New Brunswick

On the shingle beach off Quoddy Head
we looked for sandstone streaked with quartz,
miniatures of those that rouge the ruins
of Iona, another quaintly-peopled island,
also pocket-sized, exactly east of here
where we spent several months before

tracking Christian saints and Celtic kings,
histories inherited, sins earned.
Then, before my eyes an osprey dived.
We said we'd lived together long enough—
at least I said it, tracking it in your eyes,
pocketing a few last sedimentary things.

(As once before, when September's moon
floated full across the deep bays
of our front window, the noon sun bobbed
in the tide-slick like ice in January.

Sea-smoke and startled wood ducks
and morning found us at the Slough
at the mouth of the bay, the head
of what was called of old the whale-road,

in a boat lifting higher than waves,
the waves holding our sides tighter
than water, and we could see
nothing ahead and nothing behind us.

And then we got lucky. The surface
became dolphin-frothy, knitting the lace
of the sky to the Sound, and the thick
submarine knock of what I guessed

was a Minke whale passing beneath us, rolling us,
almost, as it slipped the bottlenecked
cove for open sea. For everything desperate
enough to get out rolls any stone away.)

One way or other "later" came. Heads of goldenrod
piercing the garden's side convert to flames
which a window's glass reflects. Mosses slope
to the inland ponds where each year's ice
was cut, then block-and-tackled up to the icehouse
that burned to the ground years before

I knew you. No real loss, for Christ's sake,
keeps any of us together, or apart. The things,
though, that remain require portage still, but as
memories, not things. Call mine *island window*
whale like sheets drying hard in winter air
not rolling, rolling, like those flukes of stone.

Divorce Triptych

1. *The Birds of Separation*

By morning the trees
have stopped turning. Dew
powders the juniper,

the roseate berries of yew.
Where there were,
months earlier, orioles

all over, and birdsong
like birdshot hurled
into the heat of each

new day's red start,
face down, the way
of fiddlehead ferns

now, nuthatches puzzle
the bark. In spite of all this
beauty I've been in

a callow state all morning
thinking about property
and a proper old age

and poor John Clare
who lived a long time
and enjoyed neither.

Sure my sparrows
are my own. Let ye then
my birds alone.

I see my warblers
chortling along
 burst grapes.

Just looking around,
two grackles slick
the patio's flagstones.

Starlings flock, thick
as full-grown lambs,
their jaundiced eyes

quick as machineguns.
An asterisk of blue
stars the suddenly

darkened yard
where two cardinals
whistle

come come here
back and forth
for a good half hour.

2. *Settling It*

> *It must strike most readers*
> *that a great fault of books on birds*
> *is that there is too much*
> *about birds in them.*
> —W. H. Hudson,
> *Birds and Man*

All afternoon I spoke
of it as "it" as if
for once this morning
all of it actually
came down to this

to the sandpipers' legs
moving faster than water
to the interminable
backpedaling
of gulls circling

under the moorings
tugging the fog-tails
about them or standing
apart to pick clean
the bones of the tide

The cormorants on weir posts
sat silent as hammers
their wings out flat
like butterflies
in trays of air

3. *Black Butterflies*

The sky becomes a plank
in which a nail nestles
and light the pause
that sails turn their backs to

and it settles so

or so I thought
my head snapped back
by what set it moving
I pictured myself leaving

blows unforeseen

for those one expects
the queer luck of bridges
crisscrossing my face
framing my life with you

as I always wanted it

full of property and age
and pictures of the storm
blowing safely across
the landlocked afternoons

and myself there still

standing for it all
glazed as the birdless
circles of moon on the water
or pommeling

the fat lip

of the frozen bay
like some prizefighter
mouthing my thanks
making glad motions

with my raised hands

Her Childhood

Clare in her car-seat batting
the cobwebs of sunlight
that stick to her face

only to cry when we
turn a corner
and they're gone

Broken Things

          Having lost
those early outer-space ears
to a spritely toddler's stride,
it's been *daddy dady*
daddy the sole word
roped cleanly enough
for the tongue to repeat
three times. Then,
out of the blue: *hi dad*
like the first green morning
of the spring, grass the green
of color TV in 1959
or a toplit medieval madonna,
the green of seeing green
for the first time when Monet
laid a violin like a crucifix
upon the lawn to demonstrate
the color red.
          And I am
watching from the back steps
whitecaps breaking ahead
of a toddler ready to walk
to the sea by herself
with only the name of her father
in her mouth:
          who now exclaims
in painstakingly separate breaths
daddy this leaf be broken
—and so, underfoot, a handful

of crocuses are sprouting
through winter's crust
of oak-leaf mold,
making waves at her toes.

And looking up
into the overcast
this cloud be broken
and looking down
at my sandaled feet
this shoe be broken
—a long drumroll of namings
as unbroken suddenly
as the sea's.

      Barefoot Clare,
I told myself
that day, by way of prayer,
let not your tongue be broken,
no matter how unjust
or beautiful the spill of words
you are even now learning
to break my heart for.

The Halfway Tree

Sunday afternoon, and we are off to see
    the Halfway Tree.
It's just my father and a nine-year-old (a daughter,
    mine, from this marriage)

and me. None of our mothers's here. Lost
    at the wheel, I hear
the youngest among us wondering aloud what
    a halfway tree is

half way between. "Is it only half a tree?" The one
    who, at eighty-eight, can
name all the farms along these roads according to
    who owned them when,

turns and beams and tells us how the native runners—
    Sauk or Potawatomi—
paced out the trail between the Mississippi
    and Lake Michigan

and at the midpoint blazed this tree—and then,
    in 1832,
the first American Geologic Survey
    measured it

exactly so—within a yard, a nearly antiquated
    measure now, as feet,
too, are, like these. We find the place at last
    by turning right

on Halfway Tree Road, which is clearly marked.
           Once at the tree
it takes another sign, its arrows pointing,
           to make us sure.

An orange snow fence encircles the base
           of what seems an
old, ordinarily gnarly, burr oak that doesn't quite
           stand out enough

from half-a-dozen nearby maples of nearly equal girth.
           Frankly, we're let down.
The nine-year-old: "Why did they pick this tree out?"
           She's right: were those

scouts so exact of measure? Or did some inner prudence
           doubt a maple's inner strength?
"Everything's grown up so all around." (An elder's voice.)
           "Ah yes," the driver adds,

a man of learning. "History tends to outpace time:
           the picturesque as,
say, Capability Brown planned it is already dwarfed now
           by matured thickness:

you can't see the picture for the trees (or the trees, even,
           for the rhododendrons
Empire transplanted there)." Across the street, houses
           with their prefab sheds

approach in rows, street numbers stenciled on the curbs
        in front of miles of yard.
On this side, though, where we are, half-corralling
        our tree is a real corral,

unseen before, and in the middle of it is a chestnut,
        grazing, hooded,
and a host of mottled Indian ponies, six or so, like ghosts
        of buffalo upon a field

of snow, fanning out across these Sugar River bottom
        lands like mastodons
prostrate before the last retreating glaciations.
        Facing each other,

we beam and motor off, empowered by something like
        the force of horses
turning our axletrees past all markings we have left
        down a slough of roads.

The Marfa Lights

First reported by early settlers in 1883, these
mysterious lights still defy explanation. A prime
viewing site is nine miles east of town on U.S. 90,
looking south.
　　　　—TxDOT

My daughter never saw them, but she heard
the other stories told the night before
by the *portera* in the lobby of the El Paisano
where the two stood side by side beside the blown-up
Life photos of *Giant*, filmed in the false-front
Reata ranch house at the edge of town: those
were tasty hotel sagas, of joy-cries coming
through thick adobe, of sudden cold, flickerings
in unrestored rooms—and then, later that night,
surely she thought she saw them, her own ghosts,
aglow in the corner like slices of stained glass,
which was what she was telling us all about
the next night as we drove east in a red haze
to where the lights on the southern horizon
were starting their weird do-si-dos
like car lights winding up and down alpine
switchbacks, except there are no roads out there,
let alone mountains … lights slashing like kids'
sparklers on the Fourth, fluorescent yo-yos,
knife thrusts strobe-lit, stars pogosticking
straight at us, leapfrogging the ghostlier
Charolais, the wattled Santa Gertrudis
keening the darkness before us, while this

one, this buckaroo, chattered on about ghosts
without looking where we were pointing,
without looking, even once, even for us.

The Origin of Circles

We live amid surfaces,
and the true art of life
is to skate well on them.
　　　　　—Emerson

I think more of skates ...
as annihilators of distance.
　　　　　—Thoreau

When I was my daughter's age, I learned
to ice skate on the flooded oblong end
of our long gravel driveway, a cul-de-sac
spring scalloped with run-off and rain
and my father declined to relevel come fall.

Clouds filled the ice with the washed-out
look of plastic glasses and turned into roses
wavy from so much melting and freezing over.
If the dog snarled as our scarves flapped by,
in the end we chained him to save him

from running after cars and pucks and into
the drunken sights of hunters. Then, years.
And it becomes late May in central Texas.
I enter an urban shopping mall
whose center is the only rink in ninety miles,

escorting my eight-year-old to a birthday.
She has not skated before, I only every
quarter century. How much she doesn't know
reminds me how essentials matter,
how they must be mastered, and how

I thought I once had. And today? I find
I still know how to slide, how to trust
the slippage the surface provides against
our fear of it. And here I am, at it again. …
I let myself glide out on one foot—

then, counter to all good sense, push off
with, then onto, the other. Then, again.
Then, by turns. And then I am the one
being turned, going—by what mastery?—
backwards, crossfooting it for speed,

whether lifting my daughter out of a lurch
or laying into a hockey-stop that cascades
ice-glass over daughter, dog, and dad alike—
for one moment one almost myself
back before all the circling began.

Summoning Dolphins

an epithalamion for Clare and Dane

A wedding poem or epithalamion (which is
the Greek for it) is not hard, really, to write, not
much harder, say, than "epithalamion" is to say. But
it's how to start that's difficult, and not for any
reason you might expect, such as the obviously
ticklish issue of where marriage fits in the parabolic
arc between affection and need, between desiring
and caring, between the wish to be like the one
you love and the wish to be anything but,
the radiant simulacra of true selfness,
the terrible exactitudes of mere selfhood,
knowing, as you do, how all that has been said
already, about love, about love and marriage especially,
may conquer all. All right, then. Here's my story.

You're sailing somewhere in the South Coral Sea, say
you've come there having just seen *South Pacific*
at Lincoln Center: now you are entering a narrows, which is
fjord-like, volcano-rimmed, shallow enough for the captain
to say, *Hold tight, mates, we may touch bottom*, and you spot
a fin—it's a friendly one, you're told (not all of them
in the South Pacific are), a fin, it turns out, of the bottle-
nose, the dolphin the Aborigines trained to herd
shoals of fish into their tow-rows—and a young man,
handsome in the way of mariners, a father's
true son, tries summoning more of them, beating his hand
again and again on the hull of the catamaran.
But today this text-messaging of the human
speaks to no porpoise. Even the lone fin vanishes.

Picture now a little girl growing up in another
place altogether, who couldn't be told the kinds of things
she couldn't believe were true—how in Australia, one
might say to her, the stars are different, come clustered
differently, from the ones she sees, how water there
drains in the other direction and gum trees do not grow
the kind of gum balls she can chew, how a dolphin
is a mammal not a fish, and therefore more like her,
with womb and lungs, than like the kind with dorsal fins.
And when at last the time came and she was ready
to relinquish the freedom of redoubtable belief
to the tyranny of evidence, her way of doing so
was to look you kindly in the eye—to smile, even—
and to say, as she turned away, *Well, all right, then.*

Dolphins live above the evidence of water.
They also live beneath the evidence of air.
They speak a language all their own, one
emitting higher frequencies even while admitting
deeper soundings. *Delphinis* is the Greek for them,
and they were sacred to Apollo, whose shrine at Delphi,
named for them, is where, in the fullness of time,
for better or worse, all sailors came who sought
the truth, although the oracle spoke to them there
only in startled cries, in delirious echoings,
in high-pitched, maimed hexameters (like these),
and often, too, in tears, the saltiest kind, those born
of joy. Well, all right, then. Listen. You may hear
the hull of today begin resounding: all of us are all here.

First Assignment

English 9
Sept 1972

The story "Last Day in the Field"
is in a pretty good way
told. It has a fairly simple

plot, is easy to read,
and is able to be
comprehended easy.

It is told by the narrator,
which plays a part in it.

*

The way the story is told
has no affect on me.
When a book is read,

it is read for pure enjoyment,
not to break down
into tiny little pieces.

If it is assigned as work,
no true meaning comes out.

*

Also, when read for enjoyment,
no true meanings come out.
You get one meaning

from a story. You say:
that is what the authors
are trying to say.

The author could be saying
something completely different.

Pedagogy

Let's take just a few
for instances. By this time next week
you may be waiting for a landau or a gurney
or a Hambletonian cart or ducking
questions under a cloud mass with a mission,
but for now there are certainly some things,
aren't there, that can be pinned down, whether we like it or not?
The foot size of snowshoes, for instance.
Who discovered tea
grew in India as well as China.
(They kept saying, "But in the foothills, Sahib,
of the uplands there grows a bush
that is very like …"
Yet who had ears?) Who even now
can hear, say, the intricacies
of internal rhyme? (Are those a few hands
in the back row?)
But no,
it's "for instances"
we want, not more conundrums,
though we mustn't underestimate the value
of difficulty, especially difficulty
overcome. A train
used to depart from this leafy station.
Now we must walk. The good news is
it rarely snows. But there's bad news:
it hardly rains either. You might as well
be in the desert, for instance, despite these few
scraps of deciduosity. Maybe you are

in a desert, tapping into cactus to wet your tongue,
like someone at a chalkboard, back turned,
all the right answers blowing in about your shoulders
their pricey consolations.

The Old School

*(On discovering that my old school—the
Aurorahville State Graded School— and the
village—Auroraville, Wisconsin—in which it is
located are not spelled the same. Of the nearby
towns named in the poem, Berlin,the largest, is
pronounced with the accent on the first syllable)*

OK, let me confess, first off, to what is
    legendary,
        the length of our vowels,
their pan-Nebraskan nasalities
    voicing corny
        jokes about driving through
diphthongs wide as from Borth
    to Poy
        Sippi to here—here,
where I'm—ah!—looking up at this last
    exhalation
        of the dawn. It is 1934
on that stone lintel
    or 1958
        when seen first by me
there, in the third grade, my daughter's age.
    Picture now,
        as I am, a Depression-era
lapidary's H, "burning a hole in his pocket"
    (my mother's wry
        way of noting an imminent
prodigality involving invariably small
    change). Well,
        it's out still, up there now,

spending its aspirated mouthful of air.
    Whoever he was,
        back then, no child of his,
I'll wager, offered him an *Olé!* from this
    state-graded
        schoolhouse. Nor from mine.
Why dawned on me only late one summer
    when José,
        my Texas friend, exclaimed,
"With your tan, you could almost pass,"
    and myself
        thinking the joke was saying
I never lived where Spanish was spoken,
    up there,
        in the rural North.
He smiled, too.

    The sign entering town
        on the County Trunk:

AURORAVILLE
Population: Unincorporated

Plosives and fricatives, aspirates not glottal,
link arms harmlessly around every vowel

of a body politic lacking even enough citizens
to count. Free radicals of concrete fleece
the banks of the old mill stream, dammed now,
a stream no longer. What was boarded up then
is boarded up yet. And what of the general
store of many doors with bins you had to thrust
your hands in if you wanted things? Today,
I had expected what? Bonsai? Kilims for sale?

Instead: me, looking up at this unedited stone,
hand in hand with my olive-silvery daughter
and hearing voices odder than kinship streaming
from the curbless streets of Redgranite their
endless vowels, labials like sudden exotica in
the markets of Berlin, faces flickering through
the black-and-white Fifties, detasseling sweet corn,
stripping cucumber mounds and vanishing who
knew how or where, their voices incorporate,
full of aspirations and disavowels as could
conjugate my unattended Chicano childhood.

A Valediction: In Memory

of the Birthday Party

for St. Ignatius

Bread Loaf, Vermont
School of English
Summer 1972

In what history now calls a "summer of blood," to party at all
    took finesse, real finesse—call it
    our backdoor miracle. We
    spread our loaves with fishes—

sockeye or tuna (or, failing that, Spam)—and laced our rum with
    "Real Coke" (although all
    original spirits in it had been
    long since de-coked).

One night the Jesuits threw two birthday parties for their patron saint,
    Ignatius, but the one where all
    might drink till dawn came after
    the Mass, and threated to leave us,

Fra Sidney from Queens stepped forth to confess, "no wine to drink."
    Which was not factually true,
    however contextually correct.
    Jugs of it there were, courtesy of

the Brothers Gallo and Almaden (those lost brands), but no drop of it
        potable, the literal spirits blooded
        by the Fathers' prior consecration
        of it, now neither trope nor nature.

Some called it unusually, almost rabbinically, tough luck
        there in those after-hours
        when someone walking off
        a mountaintop, hoping to have

counted the streaks of the evening's Perseid shower, could run
        into a Loyolan conundrum
        pitting *desideratum* against
        fortuna, the starfall

we wanted versus the moonball we got.   But can sacrilege
        be committed by mistake,
        the way a random oyster may
        fox even an abstemious liver?

Could a priest bless something—anything—by accident?
        So it was that the stout Fathers
        argued their case, slaloming
        between host and guest, balancing

the ripe pineapple of doctrine against the dull machete of grace,
        pressing the needle's eye of dogma
        into stricter crosshairs, friendlier
        fire, until the jungle-green

mountaintops of Vermont heard the voice of the law
      melt into garnets of pinot
      noir, carnelians of cabernet,
      fire opals of cool rosé,

by dint of a breath-test, *o mio Sid*, worthy of the holiest.

*   *   *

Right then, of course, ladies and gentlemen, I knew I might
      turn into a teacher. I remembered
      a poster, found one teenaged afternoon
      in England, a bloodless summer.

 I was standing at the porch of a forgettable Norman church,
      its axis not merely off-line (for,
      as you may know, all are) but
      quite wrong. I was there because

deciphering ancient gravestones in the rain had left me
      counting up all the girls I
      would never date back home.
      Beside the 16th-century

double-doors, a bulletin board announced our century's stuff:
      child-care hours, evensong,
      a bring-and-buy sale, rewards
      for lost Shelties. And there it was,

much faded—a French chef's knife beside a sliced loaf,
    goblets of claret, black as Guinness,
    in the block-print of a ransom note:
    YOU ARE ALL INVITED TO MY HOUSE.

Call what I felt then hunger if you call paychecks satisfaction.
    A *longueur*—or was it
    just being soaked through
    all that summer?—made a backdoor

in the labyrinth of this declaration open into an exclamation:
    Where faith means to leap
    without finesse. Where to eat
    means the taste of a body,

a tongue of blood. Where to enter is to go all the way in.

                    *   *   *

At Bread Loaf the faith of the Jesuit Fathers left them only
    one recourse, which, students of piety,
    they took: the profane joy of company.
    While we gossiped they unseated

from their ancient vows the benedictive stuff that leaves
    human imbibers its sulfites,
    esters, cream of tartar, tannin
    (oxidized) and unconverted sugar,

elevating their triglycerides but leaving the transubstantial
        untrespassed. And this is where,
        as we've learned to hear,
        the gears of Reformation grind

the magic of human sacrifice into the efficacy of prayer,
        which is internal and voluntary,
        converting flagellated desire
        into situational ethics.

Take my son, for instance, who is fretting out, one room
        away, Bach's first suite for
        solo cello, following Pablo,
        then Yo-Yo, two tapes,

while fighting the beginner's wish to keep the left hand
        in first position, even as the long
        line longs for bow-work
        so intricate in the right...

And now I think I may have been mistaken all along.
        (Note here the valedictorian's
        backdoor miracle: confession.)
        I may have made too much

of what was, like providence itself, merely a local adjustment
        for historical accident.
        Nor am I sure that Father
        Sid wasn't really Brother Dan

or some Paul or other from Sioux Falls. Nor can I recall
    (my worst failing here)
    the name of my best friend
    that bloody summer, a novitiate

who retreated that very weekend to a hotel in Montpelier
    to decide whether, then how,
    to get laid. Some years later,
    I learned, on the Lincoln corner

of the lane which joins the Turl and Camera, he used a paving
    stone against his own skull
    after the woman he'd left
    the Order for sent him her

four-line Dear-John letter, written both in blood and Latin.
    He ingested old Father Hopkins
    (of course), gorged himself on Joyce,
    and was drinking hard

to dodge the draft (first on, then to spite, the wings of the church).
    And so we lost touch. (I've
    lost even his name.) Why
    did I believe he had died?

When did I start seeing him, as today, seated there among you?

Unaccompanied Instrument

The violinist's fingers
are turned to wood.

Closing her arms
she closes her legs
perfectly now.

Her hands open.
Out hops a bird.

As the shades lengthen,
her hips shift. A forest
glows to its roots

and here at last,
edging toward still water,
is a path no one
has ever been down.

From the look of it,
that's how I hear it—

the wood turning
lightly in her hands
like leaves,

like leaves turning
as deer plunge through.

In the shallows
trackless minnow
sparkles scissor
their one note.

Study for the Figure of Time

So fine those hips   the muslin sheathed

the sheathing showed   how movement moves

as a fingered flute   is seen before

warm as breath   the sound is blown

     through her cool hands

Post-Conquest

—*after Graneros III*
by Gonzalo Fonseca

The taco kiosk stood on cinder blocks
which took the bluff vendor with the straw hat
three steps up to enter.

        For those days
when he took plastic, he kept on the counter
some capless Bics in a Styrofoam cup
filled with coffee beans.

        An egg-shaped
stone held the napkins down against the wind.
Rows of stacked plastic knives and forks
clicked one by one from a mylar silo

at the pull of a lever, while salsas were pumped
likewise, red and green.
                Some dripped

on a girl's sandal. She took it off, she wiped it off,
then she raised her bare bronze foot to the trash bin,
and rinsed that off, too.
            She left her foot, her right foot,

up there a moment longer, as if where you place
your foot in this world, the place it holds,
is not part of the journey
                but the glyph
by which the journey's beauty's told.

The Thousand Fragments

You say I have no new ideas. But the same words,
differently arranged, have different meanings.
As in tennis: both players hit the same ball
but one places it better, with more spin.

Deny a man wine and he will not find truth;
give him too much, the same.

Belief in God is a wise wager. Winning,
you win all; losing, you lose nothing.

Man's grandeur is knowing himself
to be miserable.
                    —from "Pensées,"
                    the work Blaise Pascal called
                    "The Thousand Fragments"

From his house on Faubourg St. Michel,
abutting a garden, between a pair of courts,
the pale geometrician turned theologian
explores the mathematical probabilities
of faith as he pursues his dream of service.

Is God a good bet? And can tennis help us
reckon it? Wagers of faith, the way the game
of viticulture meets the conversion
miracle of the grape—a trick that leaves
you tasting plum, tobacco, cherries, leather.

Which is why grapes terrify, like the outer
darknesses of space or like a drop shot
dying at your feet. That's what *terroir* does:
it frightens, as the cool blush of mourvèdre
deepens to galactic black, more like syrah.

*

When unattended by noviates,
he passes time by practicing his backhand,
the torque part, how you need to stop the body's
natural forward motion so that the arm,
rotating from the shoulder, can accelerate.

To put the ball in play, however, is the primal
oppositional gesture. For man is miserable
without God and happy only when seeking out
that Providence he doesn't know he might
possess already because he doubts it so.

He holds the ball, the racquet, and, if not
the will to win, the desire not to lose.
Tossing the ball magisterially, he thanks
God at that moment for showing how faith
in Him is not abjured by violence.

It's faith that surprises you into truth,
he thinks, thinking himself no better than
a beast trampling the vintage, his mind merely

a scarecrow warding warblers off the grapes.
Faith spares us, finesses our resistance to it,

bestows upon us words retaining breath's
lightness, as when a ball, moving, hovers
precisely because we've moved to meet it.
Or as a painting, just by standing still,
lets us see all of it at once. So: how to live?—

Real questions require a thousand answers.
If faith looks through death to see our fear
of it standing across the net, a wise man,
he writes, raising his dark glass, bets on eternity,
the odds being so much worse the other way.

And hits each ball out of reach with spin.

Le Tombeau de Paul Celan

So often perhaps in Paris one
finds thoroughfares, its rues
and avenues, are named for people.

From his last apartment
on the Avenue Emile Zola
to the suburban *cimetière*,
street names stream, filling
the text-void that is Paris
though no street here is named
for Paul Celan, no *rue* for poor
Celan. I want to cry out *why*
but who am I?—a man whose
mothers-in-law, yes, both of them,
thought him a Jew? Is it true
every poet is a yid? Celan thought so.

Most days in what was then
my 50th year of life I rode
the Métro with my daughter
to her *école bilingue* beside
the quai where that strong swimmer
Paul Celan descended to the Seine.
Friends later said he was insane
by then, by his "Seine"-time,
a word that means in English "net,"
nothing in Romanian,
and "his" (feminine) in German.
Celan rhymed it with "Rhine."

In his 50th year of life
the body of the poet flowed
beneath the nettings of the Seine,
beneath the bridge, Pont Mirabeau,
Apollinaire revered in song,
named for an ugly man known
in his own violent times as
silver-tongued, one of the new
"dismal scientists," who drank
one cheerless night too much absinthe
and died—in April, the poet's own
death-month two centuries before.

At the end of the avenue
named for the writer who
accused the accusers and defended
the Jew in an another "dark time"
(as Hannah Arendt called it
50 years ago), that crucible-
time for all that Paul Celan
called "that-which-happened,"
the poet took his leave of earth.
In all of Paris, is there still
no *rue* for Paul Celan (or sweet
Heine or noble Benjamin)?

What is an exact rhyme for
a made-up name like Paul Celan?
Is it even French? (See Kostrowitzky,
turning into some Guillaume,
residing on the Avenue Macmahon.)
Passover passed as Paul Celan
entered the Seine, swimming towards
his burial day two weeks to come
when Nelly Sachs, his *chère amie*,
would pass away. Back on May Day
a fisherman, turning a fisher of men,
bore sole witness for this witness.

There is no *rue* for Paul Celan.

Jacobus Vrel

In the room a woman sits, in profile,
looking through a door, a thing that one
can do, in Holland, when the top half's open.
Another woman, mostly arm, is framed
by shadow, *die frau ohne schatten.*
But, no. It's not Bayreuth. We want to
keep this scene Dutch, and not alone
because of those stiff ear-flapped bonnets—
it's also the dipthongs, the fruity labials,
impastoed here like strokes of light.
Dividing the room is a wooden screen
that leaves another room inside,
the curtain across it pulled back. A fire
in the hearth to the lower right seems
scarcely more than a paint scratch.
By contrast, the fire tongs beside it
are Dürer-correct, the sunspot
on the bell jar intense as the lilies
at Giverny. An ellipsis of plates
orbits the room, each the color of
full moons at dawn. The woman's chair
has sloping arms and shortened legs—
a nursing chair, it's called—and she
has fabric spread across her lap,
which at first it seems she's mending,
but no, her chin's in one hand, the other's
underneath the … whatever it is.
A quilt? Because she's chilled? Because
the door is open wide (on top)

and a fire like that can't warm a room
like this? Because in Holland sunshine's
fool's gold? Because there is so much
we can't take in—the leaf-mold smell
of nursing, say, and folded linen, light
that is everywhere and nowhere,
invisible as drapery, filling up
a room that, really, probably is being
aired out, perhaps for the first time
all winter, a room that has been signed

Jacobus Vrel

a man known to us now only
because, in an epoch we have named
Vermeer's, he signed his own small
patchwork quilt of oils like these—
a man whose story lives, as stories do,
if they do, by reaching one good
arm out, the other wrapped tightly
about its own chiaroscuro.

> *After the painting usually called*
> *"The Little Nurse." Nothing is known*
> *of the artist besides his signature*
> *on some 30 paintings.*

The Art of Somnambulism

*Caillebotte's boulevards were populated with
elegantly clad figures strolling with the expressionless
intensity of somnambulists.*
          —The Web Museum, Paris

In the expressionlessness
of real life when the barking
began he remembered the
taciturn thin Limougeaude
Christine fingering her hair-
shirt of prayer remembering
himself wanting only what-
ever that shirt of hers were
it ever to unsnap or
unbutton or come unsashed
(or however it is hair-
shirts get undone) would hold out
for him for yes he wanted
to hold her breasts but not the
way Christine pursued sainthood
nor the way everyone else
seeks celebrity for his
was more like a bag-lady's
need real but with limits
like the year jasmine flowered
all January until
winter arrived at last like
a misery he could paint

Stripped to the waist thickening
the foliage with his brush
he cut the sky in on his
knife stroked the landscape aglow
until the light seeped away
dropped off the edges and he
knew at once then it was not
a shirt at all but a dress
a pleated one and that their
two shadows had crossed under
the pier the very one they
once walked out on when they
took the train to get there
surprised at so many people
so well-dressed walking out
in the rain but the water
was already painted out
parasols become walking
sticks and then he was thinking
not of Christine but the Gare
St.-Lazare's steam gathering
as the new century was turning
its pentimenti building up …

and then he added the dog

Assignment: Drawing Water

*for Margo Sawyer, who uses this
assignment in her first-year art class*

Water does that

        assuming

    the shapes of

          other things

     even when

       drawing

   to a level

        all its own

     it's one

  kind of trick

        we call beauty

    That's why we

      love what we can

        if barely

   understand

     like water's

       filthy

      green sky

before a hurricane

Pine

Moon dismantling through my limbs

I remember how lightning
touched me, how I darkened

to the cool smell of my forest,
the color of flowers,
these scarred fists.

*

I knead roots into the loam
like thumbs. When water
strains at the knot, I groan
like an old man in the wind.

Where sun cannot bend
low enough to touch me,
I lay arms down with my brothers.
For what grows sharply falls softened.

*

Come, bed under me.
Speak. Level with me.

*

I have followed
the praise of axes,

ring after ring,
bowing at every stroke.

Already I am everything
I dreamed I would be.

Peonies

We open the accordion
pleats of our palms and
they hum with bees,
ants kayaking every fold.

But in the later candied
air, we turn more close-
fisted, gone the way,

these days, of theological
debates about grace
inspiring feats of charity
though bereft of faith.

Evening

As campers break open their first embers,
a boy scuttles his last summer flame
in the goldenrod beside the full woods.
They peer out from themselves, shining

like clockwork. Across the surface of the lake,
bats wing, their figures' gleam a breath
of chilled air. Out of the blue, an orange
moon licks hills into huddles lamb-thick.

A heron, more blued than blue, folds
its long neck into flight. As the light drops,
seeking the level of water, all lapping stops.
Shadow nestles in shadow, munching hay.

Onion Milk

*Chopping onions is not
an occupation which
favors dreaming.*
          —Martha Visser, *Much Depends on
          Dinner*

So let's call it one more oblique
recouping of my boyhood relish
for those late Wisconsin springs
the Holsteins gone back to pasture
in fields lathered with earlier errancies
of carrot, vetch, and wild onion

which were the weeds that were the price
of living on the land before the time
of blanket spraying with broad-band
herbicides and whose pay-out was
a greasy whiff of sourness in the milk
a gunbarrel chill against the palate fine

or so one late night I remembered it
handfuls of dripping onion wedges
cut Chinese-style tossed into a well
oiled and now steaming wok
my eyes still blinking long after
the hot metal stopped spurting

Bifocals

April. It's April again,
its flag on the breeze
unfurling, and just as you
were wondering how to
know if you need them,

comes a second mild
afternoon in a row
settling hard against
the side of your house,
the one that is peeling.

In between shoots
of forsythia, the first spears
of spirea, what *Peterson*'s
bold caps liked calling
"confusing spring warblers"

have begun dusting
snowdrop and crocus
with Old World spices—
splashes of Tabasco,
whole spoonfuls of saffron!

And oh if only
your own palms
could rise out of this
Oaxacan bowl
having tossed the diced

and the shredded
with lozenges of
cheese nearing ripe
and wing their way
over to them, the wings

on the other side of the pane
from your lightly rinsed
arugula, and hold them
OUT THERE—in focus
now like a koan

because turned from,
seen into because not
seen through. But you
can't, see, after seeing you
move at the window

to turn the tap off
now the whoosh
of water has already
spooked them,
the ones with wings.

Once more, then, silence
and the evening's greens
draining and a window
winter has left its
handprints all over.

Midday, Midsummer

All morning the wind
blew rain out of the black
trees now a weave of sun
waves across a wall
of nandina vanishing
like a ball it's so bright
cicadas start winding up
their missionary pitch
a quick overcast and the
eyes have it a welcome
shade by the pool side
into the shadow of which
the shadow of a tiger
swallowtail lurches
giantly light as a bat.

Daughters of Proteus

*(To Renaissance mythographers, it seemed reasonable
that Proteus, as paterfamilias of the entire mutable
world, should himself father a bevy of beautiful
daughters.)*

Even when asleep I hear them pitch
against the cliffs, lapping the rip-tides
like seal armadas torpedoing waves.
Sporting the wall-eyed smile of those who keep
instructions to a T, one jerked me free
of sleep: I fielded each question with my body. ...

Before my eyes arose the sort of cocky runt
whose wife's a wench. I came and went amid a maze
of gill and muzzle, tortoise-shell and mane.
Flagging, I turned tail, heaved, and, gloating, sighed.
I watched his eyes watch mine as seamen do and paid
the price of all my wise-ass answers with a wing.

I bided time, became, in time, as handsome
in the night as anyone. I saw his eyes
say when and I transformed the dark in them.
All that there was left I changed, turning myself
into his wife. My brain burst into fists
of bloom; my sockets hummed beneath his thumbs:

new flesh unpetaled from crushed bone.
Breasts filled his palms. Two thighs arose,
unzippered from the salt sea-chill. Ring after ring,

my waist met his. A woman's words slipped off
my tongue: I am in Ilium with a Parisian.
Watch your ass. Now laid in foam, now drying

in the sand, I dug for cherrystones to feed my own,
my several daughters, who would be ranging, blond
and feverish as starlight when the morning caves
between their legs and night turns outlaw
in their arms. And then, lips buttoned, how they
     change—
sleepwalking to the arms of anyone.

Sister Noire

—for Sister A-M
BLSE, 1971

There is a certain danger coming
back to it like this after so long
the cabin in the woods filled
with women emerging each morning
without their habits most of them
without even their veils making
their way among us so who could tell
who was in service to which vow
or what it looked like in practice

this one my favorite

whose long red hair came to an end
in easy curls whose easy laugh
took all derision out of laughter
no piece of jewelry whatever
just one small cross no bigger
than a button on a vermilion
chain so slight I only saw it
fast on her flushed throat
when we stopped dancing

Vermont

I regret not having fine silk of ten-foot length
To paint the Yellow Mountain pines.
Picking up at random a half-sheet of paper,
I splash ink, and hoary dragons rise.
> —inscription by Hua Yen for his
> painting "Huang-Shang" (Yellow
> Mountain Pines)

Do I alone remember how it left
calluses, writing? Pressing a ballpoint
firmly on lined paper often left me
two—one on the inside first joint
of the second finger, the other on
the outside second joint of the little one.

These were reminders. They said:
you are not starting from scratch
the way other pens besplatter ink.
Your beasts are not stroked. They
are squat and hard. Like the way each
clock last night hurt all the way through.

But then, by morning, I'd pulled in here,
my dark corners squared and tucked under,
the Green Mountains leaning out,
leaning out the way they do, out of
the blue, themselves peppered black
and blue by spruce and tamarack, ham-

hued maples, scrambled-egg birch.
In a far field three horses, each the size
of fingers, hold the hillside still
for dawn to write on. A screen-door slams.
The woman who steps out, stretching,
is beautiful, not like a swan whose wing

can easily break a man's arm, but like
my daughter, nearly a woman now,
with blue tints of her own, who is
doubtless growing daily into the arms
of emperors who want to tell her how
she will find her own peace long after

the one who dreamt of conquest once,
has left on his yellowing half-sheets
the roiled battlements of a name.

Afterwards

Reading it just now I knew
they had started, the slippages
one must learn to expect,

those common places
it is commonplace
not to place too precisely.

What I read about
was you. That you had died.
What I remembered, then,

was how surrounded we'd been
by all those ducks, the green
air faintly fair but failing,

as we talked of how many
vectors lives at twenty could
take, how joy shakes so

many hands before going
indoors. We were tossing
crumbs onto the redolent grass

and into the smoking lake.
You spoke of how the unexpected
pregnancy possessed you

with alarming liquidities,
of how you loved him and
would join him after finals,

and yet you seemed to be tossing
in the air wine glasses that never
landed on any floor you'd walk

barefoot across for the rest
of your life. That's how
you put it back then, your voice

grasping the gunwales
of your next half-century
for which we had become

odd spectators, you and I,
two old people who don't stop
speaking just because someone

else is speaking, and so we
ended up kissing. Not
the kind of kissing one

kisses so as not to
talk any more, hoping for
something more, but

only to stop talking. Up, then—
but it happened so much later—
from that duck-muddle

arose this new sense:
just because something happens
doesn't make it true, only real.

Ground Wars

Fresh on the heels of another wound-red
sunset gone hydrogen-peroxide frothy,
my friend came striding fresh from Chicago,
barefoot across the manicured grounds
of Immaculate Heart, a shaft of leftover
moonlight taut as a brown trout hooked
or a dowser's wand biting the dust;

his "Creative Rotting" rugby shirt unbuttoned,
all hair and heart, his pockets stuffed with stash,
balloons, and the whole amazing Duck family
in high-impact plastic and a skeleton
that lifts from its coffin to take the wooden
nickel you've slipped it under the shroud ...
when he was stopped by the cops and frisked.

Call it trespassing, call it bad luck, but in this
ventricle of the heart of Texas men with badges
don't cotton to anyone without shoes looking like
somebody without an ID, and so they booked him
there where he stood, the Raleigh and St. Augustine
grass sprouting beneath his foot-soles, the lariat
of his good word twirling in the sultry air.

As they pressed his fingers in ink, he listened
to the far-off up-and-down sluicing of the long
Gulf coast of night. Released on his own
recognizance, he stood beneath the I-road
and watched the whole length of MLK bleeding
beads of red and bat-quick headlights scratching,
on our hard-edge Texas nightlife, stars.

Like Hershey's for Chocolate

The slipp'ry seat betray'd the sliding part
That press'd it, and the feet hung dangling down.
        —William Cowper, *The Task*, originally
        The Sofa

I am reading of bombs that are today
pummeling Kandahar, seated on what
in my parents' house was called a davenport—
a brand name, I now know, for a new kind
of long sofa, like Hershey's for chocolate.
And it was on (meaning "about") such a
familiar item that the famous (in his day)
author of the "Olney Hymns" was asked
by Lady Austen, who was seated, perhaps
reclining, on one, if he would write her
a new long poem on the subject of … a sofa—
which is exactly what this obedient lover
of wild leverets did, entitling it *The Task*,
giving his own labor its new brand name.
"A daisy cutter" (I'm reading here) "will
incinerate everything in a 600-yard swath
and with enough sonic force to collapse
their underground caverns"—and a swath
in my parents' time was a word for work
still often done with scythes to lay out grain
not by but into shocks. Am I listening
to the sliding parts of what we say become
brand names for what will no longer hold
our weight …? And should it be only words

weighing my thoughts, as I strip off the back
of the sofa, for my cold feet, my mother's own
crocheted, flamboyantly striped (in colors
nature has no words for), moth-pecked afghan …?

Civilities in Time of Civil War

And through it all you were transposing

in your head one of Falla's difficult farrucas
for cello, trying to recall where your brother
sat upright compiling his list for the Party

beneath the lamp's swinging buoy.
Your faces flushed by the same low light,
you remember how the two of you brushed

accidentally on the shoulder, and, later on,
in the "impact studies," how the victors
would unfurl, now this way, now that,

the gainsayers from the vouchsafers,
would prefer "taking umbrage" or "seeing red,"
and then lose sight—again perhaps for ever—

of how close everyone came to embracing.

Visiting the Somme

Seven days of bombardment—
from artillery only, not the aerial
ways we do it now—laid more
ordnance than in all human
history up to that point, though
"that point" is as antiquated now
as shillings or talents,
Deutschmark or franc.

Measure being temporal,
on the eighth day, which was
in fact the tenth—for, owing to
bad weather, two bombing days
were lost (like the planned
walkover, even time at that time
turned into a death march)—there
occurred the greatest loss
of military personnel
in a single day of warfare,
ever.

La forte somme—meaning
top price, or not what is
de bon marché at the local
marché. And the Somme
today? On the map it is

straight but slow and old
and green when traced by foot,
not taking a *somme*, a nap,
but lazing through market
and village no older than
market and village in,
say, Newfoundland. Over here
les arbres d'alignement are
chestnut now not plane—third-
growth at best, morel-like
leafage punctuated by ornamental
mountain ash, dotted with holiday-
jolly, red, inedible fruit among
roadside stands of *pêches*
jaunes (not yellow sins or
péchés but white peaches)
all the way to the neatly
boxed cemeteries of white
chocolate wafers arrayed
upright like a luncheon treat
served on a trencher.

    Tout fait somme,
everything counts, as Siegfried
Sassoon, the "line-master" who
went "over the top" more often
than any other, told Wilfred Owen
as he lay not dying once more
in Craiglockhart:

              "Rhythm
is literally zigzaggedness,
not like water flowing but like
flow impeded, water over stones.
So rhythm undercuts meter
but offsets rhyme. Which is why,
old sport, we turned a good old
English word like *rime* to *rhyme*
so as to 'rhyme' with *rhythm*
which is Greek not English."

"Gallipolli," Owen sighed.
"It's Gallipolli all over."

And to his mother:
"I have not been at the Front,
I have been in front of it."

    And now it's impossible
to find level ground anywhere
you walk on this battlefield,
to go out on even such a blue
midsummer noon as this one
—as blue as that one—
without losing your feet,
without mis-stepping,
though fences keep you
from entering fields of
ordnance still unexploded. …

Somme toute. Let's say
it means "when all is said
and done." It hits you only
as you leave small towns
like these in France
and the road sign
draws a red line
through their names.

Cliff Tombs: Pinara

It's a bare smile, under that floppy
baker's cap, worn bergère-style, cropped
almost by the top of this photograph.
Your white sneakers wore out Oxford,
Istanbul, and Maine that long, long
summer. Can you be in diapers still?
A handsome man, now about my own
age, named Alexandros, whom I later
tipped silly, carried you on his shoulders
up the cliff tombs of the kings and stood
you atop the broken, heart-shaped
pedestals of what the guide book called
the Temple of Aphrodite, half-buried
in the pines. You looked down into empty
funeral crypts and down the steeply
terraced valley planted by the Romans
where sorghum grows now instead of
poppies. It is June in Pinara, almost noon.
You are the hottest, blond, not quite two-year-old
in all of Ionia. Alexandros wrings out your bonnet
in a foot-wide, foot-deep mountain stream
moving through rock as opalescent
as the porcelain drinking fountains in town
I called "bubblers" as a boy. Water
runnels down your temples until you stop
crying long enough to smile, then cry again.
In this fir glade, the earth is glazed
the red and black of museum ewers.
A Turk with a Greek name, Alexandros

tries explaining Ottoman history to us
in his pidgin German. As he speaks I follow
the flight of purple butterflies, iridescent
as the hoopoe's epaulets farther up the coast.
I find I have four pictures of the theatrum—
its perfectly preserved bowl held
the whole male population of the polis—
five of you, two of Alexandros
holding you, three of empty
indistinguishable tombs, and one
of your mother changing her shoes.
Years later I find myself writing all this down,
remembering the scowl on your face
like the gutturals of some oracle
as we dropped down the corkscrew
passage from the cliffs in our ancient
eurocompact to the deforested
Anatolian plains, and the sight
of Alexandros, our own private Hermes,
waving goodbye in Turkish now,
gule, gule—"go laughing, laughing."

Allianoi

Propitious Queen of Love; …
All Nature is thy Gift; Earth, Air, and Sea:
Of all that breathes, the various progeny,
Stung with delight, is goaded on by thee.
            —Lucretius, *De Rerum Natura,*
            trans. Dryden

Istanbul got us almost used to it—
the shouts of frenzied young men in the street.

Elsewhere, every flattened slab of stone
seemed one time or other to have been

an altar, each oil-dark heap of rock
one step nearer the history of a sect.

But then on a hard-edged tanzanite
afternoon in June we came to a new dam site

ruled in antiquity by Hera
but now by Turkish Electric Power.

The winding paths to the baths
on stone-laid footings both

Roman and Byzantine
shadowed by new, mythic-sized, still-to-be-strung pylons

were awaiting the inundation
that was a cause for "political action"

in Istanbul. Scaffolding
surrounded the hot springs,

roofed over by the same hard translucence
that covers back porches back home in Wisconsin.

Inside the walls, all transportable
artifacts had been transported

long since, just in case,
to a *müze*

in the nearby town
of Bergama, the ancient Pergamon,

whose library "lost" Aristotle's treatise on comedy
rather than "lend" it to Marc Antony.

(The librarian buried it
and the grubs got it.)

The artifacts remaining here are only
copies, but they are plenty

talismanic still, assuming you've not forgotten
how to be amazed at how craven

we can be. Here still, at the source
of the caldarium, stands a life-size

statue of the goddess whom Lucretius
called the *genetrix* of all things propitious,

nourishing and fruitful, *alma*
but *voluptas* also, giver of joys more raw

and wounds more dire
than even those of war.

The mineral springs still flow,
torpid and clear, casting a green glow,

while upstream the earthworks rise
which will turn these baths into the price

the underdeveloped pay for what we,
the overdeveloped, call priceless: energy.

And "energy," according to Lucretius,
was *Alma Venus*, who, although she's

only cast in plaster here still holds
in her cupped hands, before her *mons_*

veneris, her famous half-shell,
well-patina'd, with an egg-ripe smell,

in which the healing waters, bubbling still, still drip,
where the Old Ones came to lave and sip.

What We Thought We Came For

I couldn't remember and you couldn't either
what left us so distracted, or were we just
sunstruck, leaving the bright coast at Fethiye
for the drive south and east and then deeply
inland, into the Turkish chaparral
looking every bit at first like ours
in Texas, all scrub cover but without
anything that could even pass for a tree
like a mesquite, and then all at once there
they were—tall, drapey pines like Douglas fir,
and then the ground went bare again, then turned
as red as Laredo clay and then was blanketed
as if it had been planted, with trees, every-
where trees, low and gnarly, forest-like
(though one you could see clean through like a scrim),
trees thick with green, almost leathery leaves
which when the wind turned them shook silvery,
and then a lake, a very large lake, large
enough to throw combers up, was arriving
on our left and kept on going as far as sight
went but with no sign of any people, no
boats, no shoreline developments,
and no roads even, only this lonely
unlined four-lane, divided motorway,
its surface blemish-free like buffed travertine,
and without shoulders either, nothing edged,
graded or graveled but merely deep raw
culverts along both sides, sometimes with rusted
machinery tipped on their sides inside them

like road kill but on a road too new
for that or mileage signage or power lines
or, oddest of all, we suddenly noticed
(as when back there you turned to me
and said that maybe olive-colored leaves
might mean they're olive trees), too new
for cars also, for we had not passed one
in what?—more than forty kilometers—
before we left this phantom of a road
cemented into its new economies
of scale we had no way to fathom (as
is often how we find ourselves in Texas
also), and then we turned at last onto
a quick-rising, rut-filled single-track
and back into coast-light but powdery, fainter,
where what we thought we'd come for
hovered like a horizon that brought up close
the high sarcophagi of twice-doomed Xanthos.

The Eagle Owls at Crow,
A Bird Sanctuary Near Ringwood
on the Road to the New Forest

At least since the Forest was named in the eleventh
century, and well into our own, eagle owls, the
largest in the world, were native to this place.

And they could live here even yet, in what's
left of the wild, though in the wild they kill
everything that comes within their range
of more than twelve square miles, from vole
and stoat up to songbird, dog, and even small deer.
And, like dogs, they mark their sites with urine.

But it's their dogs that those who do live here
can't stand losing to such systematic assassinations.
Therefore, Crow—its rows of deliquescent quonsets
resited from the last war to this pig farm derelict
since before that. There is a well-stocked man-made
lake nearby, two herons, common gray ones,

going somewhere overhead, and a pair of kestrels—
one performing, bells on her legs, flying apart
from the other, wild one perched on a line
over Overflow Parking, eyeing winter wheat
turned white by gulls. Love things hard enough
and even a bird feeding may be a rehearsal.

Near Surfers Paradise

Gold Coast, Queensland

Yesterday dawned over a sea as flat as land
Waves slippered in turning white as sand
The horizon line so light it might spell rain

Hard rain tonight fell louder than the surf
Felled palm fronds piled up in windrows
Resurfacing the blue courts of Park Lane

Heads atop boards bob in the noon's neap tide
Through calligraphic foam surrendering their ride

Swansea Bay, Old and New

From 1716 copper was smelted in Swansea,
leading to copper sheathing, the greatest
naval advancement of the day—wooden
ships whose hulls did not rot.

I.

The copper first
smelted here then
keeled so all
Welsh barques
named for Greek
letters or novels
of Fenimore Cooper
ruled all seven seas
until the timbered
town's wooden docks
burned under Göring's
aerial Blitzkreig

II.

Far from buskers in
their subways of urine
that fractional castle
atop the salubrious Wynd
from sands new-lined
by high-rise condos
the Head Light still

glowers toward Gower
the cockles of Rhossili
where effluvia may flow
below but still above:
Mumbles by moonlight

The Devil's Rosary

But the world cannot dispense with stones.
They alone are not redundant. Nothing can replace them
Except a new creation of God.
　　　　—Hugh MacDiarmid, "On a Raised Beach"

The Devil's
Rosary
is a ring
of three stones
upright on
a ledge of
stone above
a slow stream
in deep woods
outside St.
Estèphe in
Périgord.
Ah! (you say)
if only
one of these
stones would move!

It is a
miracle
to find your
self standing
here in the
right place and
in the right
spot pressing
the right way
palm against
stone until
urgency
is all pressed
out of it
and becomes
like the touch

of pleasure
before it
feels the want
of friction
or seeks its
surcease for
these stones *can*
move … and yes
power is
what this is
about as
these very
large these three
very up
right stones of
what must be

some hundred
tons of sheer
lichen-pocked
granite rock
back and forth
under the
pressure of
one finger

(and yes you
can make it
stop any
time just by
believing what
moves moves
because of
you alone)

*

You could walk away from all this   outcrop
this backwash of limestone   this nearly free
fall of obsidian   an unbeliever
and find out your faith   for yourself
out there   among the leftover
pebbles of Périgord   pressed underfoot
a rosary for you to step on   along a chipped path
of veined stones   broken like oyster shells
pooled into colors   smelling of rain
the mist rising at your feet   hinting of pig shit
the flowering of truffles   or *girolles* perhaps
the more findable   nearly affordable
fungus called in English   for some reason
chanterelles   (little songs)
not "the devil's food"   their four-legged ones
are trained solely   to nose out
on our behalf   to believe in
but also to leave   for us to eat

*

It is a landscape halfway between
the central massif and the sea
Cézanne-yellow blocks of *colza*
blinding yesterday in sunlight
whited out now in sleet light

over a hill a millpond has melted
down into a field left fallow
by Corot until it has become
color without mass a haystack
by Monet the footpath that we're on
a line (barely) by Manet
walking as we are in the famed
giboulée of March the rain hard
in color hard in volume
and also in (it just so happens)
April and so I make a note
my arm about your waist to look up
"hard rain" among the storied
lyrics of every bird's spring song

       *

And what of all this
     luminous
               curiosity, what is
all this beauty, this
     spoor smoke,
            about
if not conversion—
     the way a turned field
            gets pressed under
ground again,
     the way a child
            by accident

chasing a terrier
    chasing a rabbit
        down a hole
breaks through
    the roof of a grotto
        and finds the back wall
of what is human,
    bison emerging
        out a crevice,
a cow falling,
    reindeer overhead,
        where a ceiling
dripping still
    pools
        new stone over
the blue traces of rhino,
    the pig-veined
        flesh deflecting

through the calcite glaze
    each intrusion
        of our light.

*

We are walking away from St. Estèphe,
"the way by" Ligneras

as they say in French
(see Proust) and out we come,

out of the rain, onto a road so ancient
it's a meter below ground, with four

stone steps going up out of it here
onto the edge of a plowed field

beside a square and tree-tall
power pole of poured concrete.

When Pound walked this way
he saw figures form out of the mist

like stones, planted in the ground
of their own voices, singing. ...

This morning, though,
by the oyster light

of the unslandered dawn
each new day banks on,

it's just you walking
beside me, the clouds

low enough to step on,
the world too wet to pick,

the pigments of the actual
maintaining their fine

line between us, limning
the promise of immanence

as if we'd become
the drawings underground

blown onto wet stone
through a bird's bone.

North of Austin: 1980

1.

Driving central Texas rarely
invites archaeological inquiry.
Soon there will be many, many
lanes where now are only four,
plus the shadow one, on one
side only, itself only two lanes,
and on only one side of *its* sides,
trenched for run-off runs a fence.
This, the I-road's off-road,
once the whole road out here,
skirts at freeway speed what could
be soybeans, a whole planted field:

layered pastnesses
still holding off
their becomingness

or so this, a new
thought, lets out a few
hanks of stiff rope ...

2.

Now that Temple's all that's left
in your rearview mirror
the first of the two thousand
grain silos between here and Muleshoe

lifts off the horizon like a post
we once hitched all horizons to
and then the exit to Troy Auto
Salvage ushers in a host of Waco
off-ramps to "Easy Frame Alignments"
(one to the Factory Bible Outlet,

all the rest to hell) and before
long you're u-ing and y-ing
into the incoherence of Metroplex
a cloverleafage soon to be leaving
its cattle brand on every *polis*
in this land which is our land
where Placelessness will reign,
true Father of our Country,

as now the gold and glassy
high rises of central Dallas
spreading their plantings outward
begin reflecting oh say those
who still can see through one
another's reflections of one or
another vulture, black or turkey,
their gold reflections turning
like mixed couples in the glitter
of some dance hall's mirrored ball.

The Names They Found There

Whose ended *-uellos -alacz*
-byszewski when they first
came to that beautiful country
changed first their beautiful names

and then they began looking
for something to call
those mountains of trees
they found there

there were so many
and so many the same
as those in the old tongues
that had made home "home"

they found ash
they replaced elm
and the willows rose
as the pines grew

and a new generation began
planting orchards and grafting
children and dividing
each season equally

so dying would remain
a distant sound like sunlight
singing off outcrop
away from the singed

odor of clearings
and everyone who came back
fully laden laughing
all the way to sleep

may have awoke dripping
having labored all day
amid traces of snow
for their shadows even

broke out at the elbows
when they knelt down
to collect up their dachshunds
those who were far from broke

no less than those
"given to prayer"
and the mountains
shouldered a little closer

and the road spilled
its cargo of hooks
as the treeline
lost sight of the shore

far from where
industry established its forts
and soon would start
tapping gravestones

for the names of streets

"Pflugerville Faces Sprawl"

—headline, *Austin American-Statesman*

He sprays on some OFF
and goes up to the roof
to scoop out wet leaves
from the gutters his wife
believes are breeding
what's biting her at dusk.
Now the leaves of October
are falling for a second
time at the feet of his
wife, two dogs, and three
cats who are gathered
below and are giving off
by signs unique to each
species how little they can
believe of what they see.
These are the leaves that
will be left to blacken
unbagged for months
because it's suddenly
crunch-time at work
for them both, wife
and husband: *but things
won't stop spawning*,
each reasons, exultant.

There's a place somewhere
where the fall is turning,
not making just another

wrong turn off the I-road
toward the capital and finding
nothing there but Democrats
who call all this up here
"sprawl"—this realm of cat
and coyote, of deer ticks
and fully preventable
heartworm, where everyone
is on amoxicillin,
zinc, and gin, and so
in love they'll do it, all
of it, all over again.

Way Out West

51st Street and Berkman

Bicycling west toward the freeway
less than a mile from your house
you come upon some letters weathering
in polished granite facing the ghost
of an airport from the corner of a park
and all within sight of the Capitol

where a settler stopping here for water
(a dry creekbed still depresses the bull-
dozed landscape away from the monument)
was "stabbed & scalped by the Indians"
(it was 1832) while "surveying lands
for the colonists." He lived a dozen

years more, dying in Bastrop, "a true
patriot." That's what the sign says, etched
in stone, as truth is, and just as few stop to
read it as any poem. You don't. You turn
here—what?—maybe three times a day, but
who is ever on foot (or looking even now)?

As wind strums the high-tension feeds
to the PROMISELAND of the nearby World
of Pentecost, a faded pennon crying 6 PAX
* BLOCK ICE encircles a U-Totem: flycatchers,
scissor-tailed ones (remember, you are still
looking up), bulk up here before moving on.

In This Our Neighborhood

Once known all over the city
for its offal—hock, ear, trotter, heart—
our Foodland was shortened to FKB,
then hopefully offering catfish steaks
and bottled *mole* sauces, and is now
the House of Redemptive Love.
The parking lot stays unusually packed.
The rest of this strip mall will, for a fee,
cash all third-party checks for a host
of discount pagers, secondhand clothes,
and day-old bread. Down the block,
next to what was once a Pay-Less Mart,
the "Pay-Less Employment Office"
has taken its sign down at last,
a kind of mercy. Sleet has stripped
the boughs of mistletoe from the crowns
of trees, strewing the ground with green snow.
In their absence, every limb's an upright
public servant, impaling trash. Crack
by crack, Johnson grass inches past
the service lines on the netless tennis court
behind the Kwik Stop. It's a love game
in the maroon, black-glassed Cadillac
idling at the corner with its mink-lined dash,
its runningboard lights flashing fuchsia.
There's a * 99c BLIZZARD * at the DQ
and there's a car window going down
at the drive-through: *freakin' in the mornin'*
freakin' in the evenin' (loud,

so you can feel it in your boots,
this sole music, where the footprint
of the flight path is evolving human toes
don't ya wanna get freaky with me?
Anything hanging on a wall shakes.
"It'll freeze your brain." One by one
rows of brown sacks pass out the window.
There is a sound of corks. Champagne
pops of a drive-by—or empties lobbed
like oaths onto the deserted tennis court?
You can start to smell things adrift—
the hallelujahs and the burning rings,
the barbeque, *mi corazón*, and
all the salsas of calamity.

Fear a Joke Inside

*(It was said that Benjamin Franklin did not
author the Declaration of Independence because the
Founding Fathers were afraid he might conceal a
joke somewhere inside it.)*

1.

IN THE INDIRECTION OF HUMAN EVENTS
IT SOMETIMES BECOMES NECESSARY FOR
THE FIRST MAN TO MANAGE A BOLD HAND
EVEN A MAD KING WOULD NOT MISUNDERSTAND.

2.

Warming his feet by the stove,
    he sees a possible republic
take the shape of his mind,
    fashioning a country of invention

into flakes of fire taking shape
    about his feet. His declaration, then,
will constitute a chronicle,
    not of heaven on a hill

but of a reasonably good man
    in a reasonable land, like this
room, this fire, this armed
    rocker, which is wholly his.

3.

Well-heeled but with an honest streak, a proper
Printer and a prince's welcome guest,
Lover of women, fondly tied to none,
Who reasons with the best and counts his change,
He remembers the rain and pokes the fire.
Learning at last to be humble, he writes about the sun
Setting and rising on the President's chair.
The spectacled eye recalls the storm,
What natural threatenings of the air
One does and does not expect to be
Struck by, earning in the end, through the lightning,
The peace of holding on, listening for fear
Inside. In his own small hand he invents
The state of his mind, a self-evident
Commonwealth, innocent of weather.
Laurel stars the slopes of his capitol;
About the veined walls of his chambers
The history of the nation is printed in smoke
As his finger moves through the ashes
Like the shriven tongue of an Indian, and his ring
Makes a little light through all the belled corridors
Like a key on a string, bearing the inscription of fire.

Ralph Waldo Emerson Visits the Fenway, 1880

*Suffering secretly from Alzheimer's, he's taken to see a
real-estate venture in an undeveloped part of the city.*

He never liked coming into Boston
just to visit. To lecture, yes, of course—
or to buy books. But this time took him
to where he'd not been since, a year later,
he fixed his eye again on his wife's corpse.
(He was young then, a man who kept a journal
and wrote: "Visited Ellen's tomb, opened the coffin.")
This latest visit found him in the last place developed
in the city, a region some still called the Fen,
where the old Unitarian saw not swamp but
what he once called circles, though they weren't
circles exactly, more like squares turned on end
trying to fix a foundation firm enough
to build a city on a hill on. What he saw
moved like a game, visitors gathering uniformly
in circles round a square, a square like some
green jewel beveled, with other people coming
from as far away as Providence
or Portland, visiting this game like a
museum. Those who congregated did not
come just to watch. They came to talk and visit,
to tell each other stories of the fabled
history of Boston when Massachusetts
starred as the only commonwealth,
with libraries, universities, even poets—
men with three names apiece who shared

a sense of purpose bright with Anglo-Saxon
ruth that comes from looking the remains
of death in the face. "New York is a sucked orange,"
you might have heard them mutter, had you
been there, visiting, scouting a place
to be seated or build, as names quite unlike
his materialized, filling the tumescent air
like magnets on a fridge, or flags like socks
unfurling on a pole, like fossil poetry—
Pesky   Yaz   El Tiante Big Papi Tony C

Another's Brass

*always on the limit, trying to get into business and
trying to get out of debt, a very ancient slough,
called by the Latins* aes alienum, *another's brass, for
some of their coins were made of brass.*
>—Thoreau, *Walden*

*I do not clean my brasses half as quick without the
accompaniment of his flute.*
>—Ellen Sewall, the great unrequited love
>of his life, on the subject of Henry

What "the Latins," he says, identified as brass
was often bronze—the issue being
what it's an alloy of, how much copper
versus how much zinc, how much tin.
Or else by "brass" he just meant copper,
a true element, plain and simple.
But there you have it: patinas, usages.
For Americans, "brass" can mean the moxie
it takes to pull something off, like a deal. Or,
the officer issuing orders, dressed in stars.
For Thoreau, alloyage was an American legacy.
It was how his Puritan ancestors had been taught,
thanks to the native lore of "the Indians,"
to seed fish while planting furrows of corn.
Thoreau told his contemporaries: plant oaks
among pines, pines where there are only oaks.
He put the spices in his steamed rice
whole, a lesson learned when he opened

a squirrel's cache in search of the origin
of seeds. A man who knew economy
and wrote a chapter on it, he foresaw
a marketable alloy in the fusing
of graphite and clay in a cedar sheath.
(Though it's become a has-been now
thanks to new hybridities, I confess much
of this was writ with that elder fuse still lit.)

From his day to ours we have lost
nearly seven varieties of wild apple
every year. Sweet corn is so hybridized
it would cease to exist if humans stopped
cross-pollinating it. We can still,
perforce, be moved by a great tree felled.
(Last year a college student, protesting
a Weyerhauser-clear-cut fell out of one.)
The same year Thoreau graduated from
Harvard, Darwin returned from Galapagos,
having seen virtually identical finches
some eating seeds that others couldn't.
Back at Harvard, Agassiz held court,
basing his case for geologic cataclysm
on fish bones. In front windows the new
border war spoke the lingo of local politics
as Concord renamed its Main Street, Texas.
(So partisans for the other side lobbied
to rename my Wisconsin hometown, Mexico.)

Justice survives its allegiances, beauty
its benisons, as swallets drain pools of
subterranean limestone. Fauna
perambulate whereas flora exfoliate.
Brass: it all came back to you, as you
lay dying, Henry David (and how do you
pronounce that French alloy of a "Thoreau"?)
while sister Sophia seated at the window
read aloud your own words to you, narrating
the seventh day, sailing on the Merrimack,
how it seemed to enact Creation's last day,
with you and brother John together,
almost for the last time, whether tacking
to windward or riding tantivy on the current,
streaks of oil pellicular as milkweed
traces on the suddenly frosty air.

It all came back to you, in that alloy
your words fused, sheathed in Sophia's voice:
how "brass," like all of us who come from elsewhere,
is always *alienum*, made up of other stuff
becoming still other stuff, however randomly.
So Ellen would polish her candlesticks, a good
Puritan, plain and simple, who "abjured"
(this was Emerson's coinage) every eligible
male Thoreau, but fused all her good works
like a Greek lyric to the sound of your flute.

—WRITINGS WITH OTHERS—

Texas

—from Jorge Luis Borges

Here too. Here, as at the other end
Of the hemisphere, an endless plain
Where an unheard cry of alarm dies out.
Here too the lasso, the Indian, and the colt,
As well as the bird, itself out of sight,
That is singing over the roar of history
Just to keep a single evening memorable.
Here too the mystic alphabet of stars
Dictating names to my pen the ceaseless
Labyrinth of days cannot efface: San Jacinto
And that other Thermopylae, the Alamo.
Here too, then, so anxious and brief,
That inscrutable thing we call life.

Ronsard's Complaint

—from Pierre de Ronsard

When even candlelight has begun
to show how very old you've grown,
spooling and spinning by the fire,
you might be mouthing to yourself

some line I wrote once, then look up,
a bit surprised, and murmur, "Oh
that Ronsard—how he praised me so
back then"—when, startled at my name,

your girl, who had been dozing, cries out
a blessing on your own. Myself? I'll be
long dead, one of the myrtles' boneless ghosts.

And you? Almost so.

    The roses of life!
Pluck them all, quick, now, at once—
there in the dimness where you work
regretting love, your fierce disdain, my art. ...

To Rimbaud

—from Paul Verlaine

It is raining lightly on the town
—Arthur Rimbaud

My heart cries out
The way rain rains down.
Where did it all come from,
This heart-lancing sound,

This gentle bruiting
On rooftop and ground …?
To a heart that is pining
Are raindrops its sole song?

To a heart that's lost heart
Is there no betrayal,
Just tears without rhyme,
Loss without reason?

But worst by far is
Not knowing why, free
Of love and hate alike
Grief still overflows.

What Remains

—from Horace

Run-off snow is prodigal bequeathing a meadow
        returned to grass.
Swollen a moment before the rivers now
        abide by their banks
though the chains of the earth have been shaken.
        Thaw follows frost
and spring turns on its heel becoming summer,
        while summer shifts
from foot to foot the blast of autumn's brilliance
        stiffens in winter's joints.
The earth, you see, moves as a woman moves
        naked in the company
of women. At evening it will have dawned on us
        that it was afternoon
all day. Old moons will open wounds
        new moons have healed
but once we have joined Tullus, Ancus, Aeneas
        and the rest
even these ludic tropes will be dust. ...
        How long we have got
we can only say: *than what we want*
        a little more,
a little less. When you see Minos, my friend,
        stepping from the shadows
to mark you for his own, the bottom line is
        yourself alone—
not what you've done nor hoped to pass on.

        Remember Hippolytus
who, though chaste, was tossed beyond even
        Diana's outstretched arms.
Remember Pirithöus, would-be savior of Persephone,
        whom Hades rewarded
for his labors with a throne of adamantine
        chains, and Theseus,
too, remember, who vainly tried to save him,
        his mule-hearted friend.

Ecstasy

—from Victor Hugo

And I heard a mighty voice
       —Book of Revelation

One starry night as I was
watching the waves alone
not a cloud above no sail
upon the sea just looking
took me it seemed deeper
than things as they are
as each part of the whole
appeared to query randomly
how the high places flamed
how the low places flowed

and then the golden stars
in battalions numberless
bowing their fiery crowns
all spoke in voices hushed
or else fortissimo but still
in harmony just as below
that blue surf which no force
subdues or steers declared
on crests of curling foam
This is your God, the Lord of Hosts

The Moon Rises

—from Federico Garcia Lorca

At moonrise
the bells leave off,
impenetrable
paths emerge

At moonrise
sea covers land
and hearts feel
enisled in the infinite

No one eats oranges
when the moon's full.
One needs instead
green fruit well chilled

At moonrise
all its silver faces
are alike as coins
in a pocket sobbing

The Sun

—from Charles Baudelaire

It comes when households across the city
black it out with tacked-up sheets or Venetian blinds
behind which everyone's already undressing.

Now the sun's fully intent on flagellation—
of suburb and hovel, rooftop and cornfield,
architecture and nature alike. …

             And me?
I am practicing my own kind of self-
recrimination, my own weird swordplay

in which a stab in the dark finds
a full rhyme for "hazard," or a paving stone turns up
the verities in a line of verse long ago just dreamt of.

This late sun despises mists and welzschmerz, sets the infirm
texas-two-stepping on their crutches, makes young girls
swell and harvests burst and hearts flower like immortality.

When sun drains down like this
into the projects, high-fiving the high-rises,
it acts as the original televangelist

—half-prince, half-poet—

visiting hospitals and statelies alike
with the inalienable wish
of all things shabby: to be glorified.

Mote

The mote *is a Spanish form*
of a line or two. Giuseppe
Ungaretti, the Italian
poet, published in 1933
"Mattina" (Morning):

M'illumino
d'immenso

He called an earlier draft
"Cielo e mare" (Sky and Sea).

Often a mote *is followed*
by a glosa *or* retruécano
("gloss" or "play on words")
creating a chained form
like a Japanese renga.

1.

Here the motley
light shows

dusting
cleanses

dusting
coats

2.

In a mote
free eye

light becomes
the only floater

breaking sea
from sky

wearing all
the glosses

Early One Morning

—from Heinrich Heine

She's got my breakfast
Laid on, dark roast
Coffee, double cream,
My loving, lovely wife.

She pours it out herself,
Joking, flirty, smiling
With lips like nothing
Else in Christendom.

I want to say her voice
Is like a flute. Or,
Like angels. But no—
What do I know of perfect?

She is a perfect beauty.
What should be lily-white
Is. The way that hair should
Frame a face: it does.

Which is why it's odd
This morning to see that she
Could be a bit more slender.
Yes, just a bit slenderer.

Paris, 1856

—from Jorge Luis Borges

The prostration from his unending illnesses
Has so accustomed him to anticipate
His death he fears even the loud out-of-doors,
Even when accompanied by friends.
Wracked by time's river, Heine casts
Against its long penumbra the fatality
Of being human, and a Jew. Once, he thinks,
I was an instrument of limpid tunes,
But now he knows the trilling is arriving
Not from any tree or bird but from
The dire fragility of passing days,
And it's saying, no, salvation's not bestowed
Because one time you sang of golden nights
And flowers, and no, not even of nightingales.

Camden, 1892

—from Jorge Luis Borges

Complacencies of Sunday, the aroma
Of coffee and the daily papers
In which, this very morning, are published
A fellow traveler's allegorical verses.
The old man's up in bed, reading, pale
And sober as his room. He eyes his own
Otiose face in the played-out mirror
And thinks, without a trace of wonder,
That is my face. His limp hand
Grazes a blurry beard. The end
Is near. To himself he says: The "me
Myself" I now no longer am—only
A body of verses rhyming life with
Its splendors. I used to be Walt Whitman.

These Wings

—from Horace

These are not merely academic
wings. Just think of me
as bard-made-bird, giving up
the earth and lifting through

what once they called "liquid air"—
a child of poverty, a friend of the rich,
unafraid, intent only on a death
that is singular and true.

(See how the flesh on my legs has wrinkled!
Already I'm all white above, like a bird!
Soft feathers sprout even now from my hands…)

Icarus himself! And, looking down,
I chart the roaring shores of the Bosphorus;
I spot the quicksands and the gulfs of Syrtes,
the vague, deserted, Hyperborean lands.

In Colchis and in Dacia where they fear
our occupation forces, still they will warm to me.
I shall be annotated by Iberians
as long as Gauls savor Horace with the Rhone.

Epitaphs are superfluous, a waste of breath.
Dirges are disgusting. Lamentations
I lament. So just relax. Watch closely.
My funeral will be fun for all.

Ballade of Sayings From the Days of Yore

—from Raymond Queneau

It takes all kinds to make a world
It takes palsied geezers
It takes a godzillion seconds
Each thing in its place and season
Come March there's spring
A month for plucking up what's planted
One day the year ends
Winter's here when autumn's over

A rolling stone gathers no moss
A chill wind will freeze a shorn ram's balls off
Leaves of grass shove paving stones apart
Such a load of annoyance
Each tree wears its own white shroud
The sun drags its yeller butt along
After clear weather comes the snow
Winter's here when autumn's over

When you're old you're no longer young
We all lose our teeth in the end
After eating well it's good to fast
No one's contented
We miss our childhood playthings
Piss and moan about the cell phone
Those are crocodile tears
Winter's here when autumn's over

Dude, okay, so here's the rub
You're worse off if you try to argue
You've got death always round the corner
And after autumn winter

Sidecar Sapphics

—from Horace

Really, Muses mine, I know you love me. So,
let's let fear and trembling go blowing in the wind,
a sea wind, say, off Crete. Should some Muscovite
    threaten our coast

with his icy fist, or whatever new tyrant is
terrorizing the whole Middle East—it's no
worry now. Weave, you who relish
    a fountain's freshness,

weave a new garland for my celebrated friend.
Without you, all nine of you girls, I couldn't
do him due honor with this verse of mine,
    plucked on Lesbos' lyre.

Daphne: An Ode in the Pindaric Style

—Petah Coyne, her construction of Daphne: wax statuary, human and horse hair, rubber, black spray paint, wired tree branches, curly willow, chicken wire, silk flowers, bows, acetate ribbons, feathers, plywood, pearl-headed hat pins, tassels

—Ovid: "Your fair form contradicts your deepest wish."
The Metamorphoses, trans. Allen Mandelbaum

I.1

And so the Pythian Games were created by Phoebus Apollo—
    a conversion of bloodlust into sport
which begat the victory odes sung by all the lords of the lyre,
    the Grecian mysteries and Italian dances,
and all because it took Phoebus, back then, his whole quiver
    to finish off Python, a monstrous beast
from the primal ooze, his mass vaster than empires and far more slow.

I.2

On his way to the Games, his victorious locks hanging more thickly,
    more squarely, across his squared shoulders
than those of any three-ring impresario, any Siegfried or Roy,
    Phoebus mouthed off to the wingèd one,
he of the short and curlies, said to have a quiver of his own back home:
    So, what have you got in that quiver of yours
back home, big boy? Thus, Phoebus. The boy bit his tongue. Literally.

I.3

Later, atop Parnassus, Cupid's tongue still throbbing, the lad strung
his little bow, and then nocked twin arrows,
one a (+), one a (-), a resistance completing the circuitry of desire.

II.1

The second one strikes Daphne, her forehead bound in a tie-dye band,
    the kind a young *chanteuse* wears
in her early Folk-phase, hits her in the small of the back where
    her fan of black hair, innocent of the rigors
of brushing, had stiffened. *Bad hair or no* her father cries *you're far
    too beautiful to remain a virgin*, but Daphne
is already laying out guitar licks for The Lady Di's, a girl-band.

II.2

At the same time, the other shaft hits Phoebus himself
    where it hurts the most, in mid-pursuit;
when it hurts the worst, he cries out to Daphne, though she is
    already under headphones, cries out through
little mouse lips of pain and passion and what passes in Phoebus
    for persuasion: *You mustn't leave*
all that dark wavy hair of yours forever unbraided, Beauty Fish.

II.3

Now he can't decide what to do next: hum? (for nothing apt
    is happening at his lips) or stop
and pout? Winded slightly, he stops. That's when he tries wooing:

III.1

I'm not really all that bright, I know, but I have lands of my own,
    a mountain-top of powerful relations,
thousand-watt speakers, four of them, a fairly decent set
    of amps, designer drugs, a smile they'll write
lyrics of. And I love you. But she goes on fleeing, hummingbird-
    quick, gazelle-deft, hare-bent
on a hole to hide in, her Petah-puce-lava-flower locks erupting.

III.2

Turned hound-dog-mad now in pursuit of her streaming hair
    where it leaves on the igneous air heady
traces (he'll never forget what each of these words means), Apollo is
    flying faster than stags flee Apollo's arrows,
so fast he's become all god now, and he's at her shoulder, breathing
    into her hair, his moist breath finding
her ear becoming her voice praying: *Change me, Father, change me.*

III.3

Apollo leans against her trunk, vanquished. Her hair is cordage now,
    hanks of foliage. Her feet, roots. Her limbs,
limbs. *I swear I'll wear your leaves forever braided like my hair.*
    This wreath will crown the head
 of every victor in sport and song. And like my own hair, leaves
    like yours will never whiten in the wind.
Thus, Phoebus Apollo. And as the winter wind went on throbbing,
the laurel, locked in the throes of it, seemed almost to be nodding.

—NEW POEMS—

1

February. Elev. 233'

First, warmth—like a Wisconsin
late spring day dawning now across
the freeway's undertow into a marine
haze hovering astride the Marine base
while a sparrow tries chipping away
at the truth of the still lit, still full
Pacific moon, fighting off tremblors
from the down-wind gunnery practice.
The sun? It's belated, still wanting

to lour, brushing hot amber shellac
atop the chill of an off-shore breeze
and bougainvillea, which does not dip
when hummers sip, then lift off it.
Camellias shed their own rouge-light
on snowpack of felled azalea petals
as trellised full-blown American Beauties
practice parade waves toward what is
now exhaling pollen, salt, and chimes.

San Clemente

The Answer

Teacher: *Why do boats float?*
Fleur (aetat 4): *Because boats are like circles*

Boats are like circles
Circles are like mirrors
Mirrors are like kisses
Kisses are like water
Water is like sunlight
Sunlight is like circles
Circles are like boats
In which thoughts float
Where boats don't

The Granddaughter Dresses
for the Last Spring Game

Teal's their color
Cheetahs' their name
Their jerseys bear
Brand names
Town on the front
Hers on the back
An American flag
On the left sleeve.
But wait!
She's late!
The game's at half-past
She's still pink-cheeked
And red-eared from sleep
Her ginger Botticelli
Hair more tangled
But breakfast is on
First—only Tiger's
Milk this day perhaps
Stockings pulled high
Stretch pants belted
But the hair!
    The hair!
A ballet-bun
Is nixed, so it's
A pony-tail
But will the ribbons
& elastic help
The helmet fit?

Cleats come last
Of course—
     But wait!
Where's her glove?
(With the sun-screen
And neatsfoot?)
But now it's time
Fashion-plated
& ready to make
Catches she ambles
Strikingly to the plate
Hatted and batted
To end the Spring

   for Arwyn

Rain Chances

Of course
it must
be summer
since you're
dreaming how
your swing
ripped those
liners once
to right

dreaming too
how anxiously
you watched
the sky
darken with
signs you
wouldn't play
come afternoon

Were you
not dreaming
when waking
you because
you'd slept
long enough
a gloved
grandson whispers

hey Papu
wanna toss
it around …?

for Ryker

Springtime Dogleg Blues

This is a season when fissures can occur
within the town-and-country continuum
because a drought has left all the marinas
landlocked on the lake first dammed up
by desperate labor measures taken
to defeat the Great Depression but now
is a wild center of wet suburban delight.

There is a parkway to all of it now,
sporting four lanes (divided), crossing a host
of traffic lights at Nightingale Lane,
Flamingo Trot, Pheasant Run, and then
Comanche Trail. Once there were Comanches
here, who were (what is the right word?)
migrants, tracking game past the non-existent

nightingales and flamingoes, sometimes
quietly, sometimes making a lot of noise,
until Mirabeau Buonaparte Lamar informed
the citizens of the new Republic these
intrusions "through our countryside" required
"decisive action." Playing golf indecisively
at Falcon Head while trying to identity

a falcon (kestrel? merlin?), I missed
my only chance for birdie on the dogleg
by three putting. Driving home, also in-
decisively, I caught myself gazing
at the haze masking the villagescapes below.

Smog, was it? Pollen? Mexicans burning
their fields again? Or, myself, like so many,
just blaming everything on something.

Post-Op

i.m. Spenser (2005-2020)

Now that the carpenter of bone
has sheathed titanium into my
femur, lodging a ceramic ball
in a resurfaced acetabulum,
my Labrador retriever is here
to welcome me. He brings me stuff.
It's compensation, I think, for not
being quite well enough yet to
walk myself, much less walk him.

Or so I reckon Lab logic functions
as a way of linking what he's so
good at with what he thinks I need.
What I will be needing soon, I
think, is how to manage, being newly
cane-dependent, the deep declivities
of toilet seats. He brings a tissue
now, still damp, the one I used just now
to clean my glasses. I take it, thinking
of those longer, more disabled, than I.

And now he brings me today's Sports,
the newspaper coiled in his mouth
like a rope. I remember reading once
about a rope like this. Spooked by a diver
come too close to its den, an octopus
swirled its legs up and down the diver's

safety rope, turned itself rope-blonde,
closed both eyes and became invisible.
He eyes me now, this Lab of mine.
How do we envision all we need?

for Michael Adams

Mother's Laundry Was Done
in the Cellar

If she made a sound, it was never one
I ever heard those days she ironed. Did
that bespeak unhappiness? To my ears, no.
In my eyes she'd more often seem far more
pleased than not, watching in her skeptical
Swiss way (like a painter returning from
abstraction to imagery) me watching, a trace
of whatever representation she made of me,
while gingerly gripping her hearth-heated irons.

She could heat herself up fast enough
if her speaking just left others puzzling over
what she meant. Adolescence was when she lost
the need forever for what her parents spoke,
but for a *Scheisskopf* slipping out at times,
the way that starch occasionally slipped into
that heavy load her knuckles scraped, shoulder-
deep in sinks of tin, wringing the neck of farming.

Her syntax worked the way the cellar's coal dust
coated sheets. Winters, though, brought clarity
when each wet thing—undies to flannels—hung
outdoors froze hard and brightened in full sun.
Her hands would redden then like Christmas
berries, hauling in, without a word, a wash
turned skeletonic, with a smile all her own.

.

Before

Today I had a hankering to fire a gun.
No reason that I knew of, since I asked
for none. Except that in a dream last night
I acted in a play and didn't know my lines—
had never even seen the script before,
but recalled how, some days before,
the President told a very violent lie.

And then recalled, how from my teenaged
outer edges, my girlfriend asked me to
tell her if there was anything I'd really
like for her do to me, and since I didn't
know, had not been asked before, I said
"I don't know," just before she left to

join her girlfriends. Once, recalling all
those desecrated shrines in Syria, Russian
looted Ukrainian past, I remembered how
my niece's fiancé invited me to hunt doves
on the back 40 of his Texas ranch. We shot
nothing. Saw no doves. Or any other birds.

Before the hunt was over, when it was
close to 90, he was recalling, once before,
he'd shot some 40 birds one late gray
afternoon, and before all the plucking,
gutting, and dressing was done, he felt
"tired as a cemetery the days before Easter."

The only time before that that I ever used
a gun was with my dad, hunting pheasants,
sometimes rabbits, maybe a squirrel or two,
those times we still had a dog to lead,
and came to love that hickory-stocked
over-and-under .410, the one he let me fire.

And so, some months before he died
he asked me would I like for him to put away
for me "that old .410 of yours." I didn't say
I had no wish or need for any gun. Would
saying so have been unkind? Then, before
saying anything, even thank you, all was gone.

2

America Goes to War:
Green County, Wisconsin, April 1917

after the photograph in the Evening Times

Always that ashy scent in the air,
                              come fall,
But over there
On the dark courthouse lawn
                              in the center of the square,
It's a strange smell now, slightly moldy,

Like the brown rime
Of bratwurst spitting

Or the open-a-drawer-and-pull-out-what's-been-
Too-long-in-there
Odor of Limburger,
                    as at a Sunday picnic.

Streets out of sight are lined
                              with elms that umbrella them
And won't be here sixty years on,

Each street numbered, none of them named, as elsewhere,
For generals or martyrs
                              or elsewheres.

It's all part of the squaring
                    of a communal story

That got them here, now, facing this war
Facing the same names as theirs,

Where the first leaves of spring,
                                now unfolded
Greet these other leaves just starting
                        to crisp and flutter upward
In a darkness still visible

While a photographer kneels,
His face fronting the glow, hoping,
                        ambient light being the only light,
                        a long exposure of what he sees
May still see print.

Wet halloos from the few
                cart-horses hitched at the square
                        echo the scissors-rip of things being lit.

The humming solidifies into words:
                                Alles schläft, einsam wacht

Who alone watches
                is a boy
From a bullseye dormer blocks away,
His schoolbooks aflame,
                        many hours past bedtime.

American Flight

Air in Economy's gone chilly again
　　hours left to land—
　　　Captain slow to respond.

CNN's showing the dictators, Putin, Xi,
　　both nuclear-armed,
　　　faces turned our way,

Shaking each other's hand.

　　aftermath of the Ukranian invasion (2023)

Ode: Pandemic/Invasion

(In Turkish the Mediterranean is called the "White Sea")

Mouths open all over the world
                                        tonight
Trying to take a breath

Red sky at night
                            but it's redder tonight
In the East than the West
                                    a pandemic of light

To the Turks the White Sea
                                    spliced
between the Red and the Black
                                    is also the only way out

_____

On a tennis court, its net taken down and removed
                                                to stop contagion,
A couple, pink as their baby
In her stroller, are hitting balls
                                        over the invisible,

Then chase them down,
                                    their laughter spliced
Between looks at the stroller.

180

Within the yakity-yak of history,
"Times like these" are again aping
                              "times like those"

When time is a penny
          costing two cents to mint

When invasive loquats
                    squat on the courthouse lawn
Unloading their strange fruit
                    like fake news

When droplets of air
                    face off
Against the unmasked
                    surfaces of things

——————

Vaticinations from the North
Assert that now what lies
                    across their slice of the Black Sea
Has been theirs forever

And a plague on those
          who are fighting to breathe,
Unloading arms,
                    taking their shots.

3

Changing Time Zones

He doesn't reset his watch
until the plane's in the air,
and even then he fears
being presumptive

No resetting the time
she lingered so long
beneath the flowering
succulents all the bees

diverted their pollen
quests into the loose
curls of her Natur-
Tinted auburn hair.

No reset as her mouth
nearing his hovered—
a moth at the face
of a backlit clock.

Facing Pages

Translations are sometimes published en face,
the original and the translation on facing pages.

Here is what my friend tells me
what I don't remember asking:
how she will often still meet
her long-ago estranged though
now still companionable ex—
someone who can't be "eclipsed."

Her reasons are still nearby,
nearing adolescence and so
refusing to read any books
she has selected for them.
Why it is she so wants them to
read these is a worry to her,

more than a woman of forty
(and great beauty) can
put into words, because
words are what her own boys
now are using for effects
they themselves have not

yet managed to find their
own words for, and she worries
her worries are trying to want
her to turn too quickly the facing
pages of her own desires.
So, here is what I have been

wanting to answer: even if solar
eclipses follow a path of totality,
even totalities are temporary.
Revision is everywhere the idiom
of the work, facing translation
into desire, like the dinner, even

now in the oven, the one I have
invented for my sweetie, after
sifting the pantry from wish to
want to spoonfuls of the whatever
I thought would express a desire
I read in a book, not one of mine.

.

Nocturne in Search of a Key

Are your fingers long enough to play
Old keys that are but echoes …?
—Hart Crane

The notes rose
so pianissimo

it seemed less
a way of talking

than a place
to place their hands—

"taking time"
she called it

he heard as
"making time"

leaving their words
less about what is

sung rubato
than a da capo

all lovers need
to come back to

offering a pizzicati
of friction

risking a tremolo
of surfeit

fingering their
eldrich keys

casual as breakage

Recharge Zones

The van fled that crashed through the brick
wall of Greater Love, which a host of
masons from Radiant Day offered to rebuild.
Help cometh unbid, as they say, and who
is fool enough not to believe? The homeless
find hand-outs even crossing railroad tracks.
And birds, we know, negotiate between earth
and heaven by signals beyond our knowing.
But you, turning over upon a cool evening,
may easily pull the covers along with all
the lost light across you, while I lie here,
still unable to reach myself where you are,
nestled, ripe as a sun-warmed peach.

Skid Marks

I thought I's movin' fast and gettin' stronger
I thought the coast was clear
Till I look'd in the mirror
And saw a set of skid marks gettin' longer
—Butch Hancock

My second wife was married her first time
in a Canon-worthy English priory
beside a cemetery beside the sea.
Near the stone font on the west porch
where all newly weds must pass through
effigy and crypt to enter daily life,
a more-than-life-sized Pièta
cradles the drowned Percy Bysshe Shelley,
in her marble arms. Why is he here,
I thought to ask, standing with her there
in this part of her past for the first time,
a flip-book of Shelley's past skidding
across my tongue. But this time, for once,
I thought twice before I spoke, though
noticing a nearby sign announcing
the poet's heart was buried in another
church farther down the coast. His last wife,
Mary, brought it from Italy along with all
his manuscripts. I had gone on thinking
for so long that the house now was quiet.
The kids? Not yet asleep, perhaps, but
calm. I counted how many nights we two
had lain together, having both, perhaps,

the look of spouses on a sarcophagus.
Yet still, and half-like kids ourselves,
we went on, counting on nights like those
we cried all night to one another
louder than elsewhere's sculpted dead,
what we ourselves together were, we tell
each other now, so much the better for.

How Days Break

Once before,
before dawn,
when the glass
milk bottles
paper-capped
dropped off
at back stoops
from horse carts,
sparrows pecked
holes in their tops
for the cream.

Today by noon
the glories of morning
have folded up
while a large woman
waits beside her
purloined overflowing
HEB shopping cart
fighting her umbrella
not against rain or wind
of even Texas heat
but only because

like her it's old.

Walking Home
After Drinking
With Friends

I wasn't,
you know,
drunk, because
before not
much was
left I
left. Walking
was pleasant,
no need
to play
my bad
side off
against my
slump to
the right
that often
dogs my
nights. Feeling
all right,
not, you
know, queasy,
more star-
board, more
like water
seeking its
own level,
one eye

out for
rocks, one
scanning the
sky spaces.
What do
they really
mean, those
trillions, galaxies,
how many
like us?
Snow, then,
I seemed
to become,
the kind
piling up,
not just
melting away
into the
warming air.

The Real Something

May-be the things I perceive, the animals,
*   plants, men, hills, shining and flowing waters,*
The skies of day and night, colors, densities, forms,
*   may-be these are (as doubtless they are) only*
*   apparitions, and the real something has yet to b*
*   known. ...*
    —Walt Whitman

If that bird
half up a tree
newly leafed
stays invisible
its song may elate
more than that
wren you see

who is too loud
too at-your-window
for breakfast time
but its song may
also puzzle you
as public taxes do
funding private schools

and without seeing
you may surmise
you've heard it before
that invisible one
from your bed
getting you out of it
before the alarm

but you don't know
birdsong really
you're no Peterson
or Sibley though Robin
or Ayres are both
friends who can put
a name in your mouth

for many of the cries
you've heard
coming from overhead
or off the ground
or moving across
even the dearest
waters of memory

That Uncertain Something

Comes, yes, at odd times, from a
door slamming or sometimes,
yes, from a dog, a dachshund,
running, no, pulling herself along,
back legs dished out, disks blown,
her back-end belled across a
two-wheeled cart, still trying to
out a badger, no, a possum,
a cat, no, a roach, probably
a palmetto bug, the kind that
takes wing, rattling at night
a screen, a door, a shelf
of books, a light left
inexplicably on.

Texas Parable

*The Speaker claimed the President
Pro Tem was speaking in parables.*
—news report

Like two armadillos
nicked by a semi
and sent rolling
into the drainage
ditches either side
of the frontage road
flooded now from
Memorial Day storms
the two Houses
seemed to be floating
among the debris
until one struck
a drowned deer
the other a porch
railing from a FEMA
ranch house and
now both lie
(the armadillos, that is),
feet up, heads down
in the muck, as bicameral
leaders go on mouthing
their dark sayings
of clear intent.

Days of Flying Frijoles

You know, Friends, fame does not accrue
to what we do. Profit, *compañeros*,
though legitimate even for Nonprofits
like us, is not what we're after, liaising here
with forces we wish to eviscerate but need
still to respect. (You know how we've been
brought to our knees, trying to balance
mono-parental, semi-detached residences
of pulled toilets and flea infestations
against uptown comers and downtown shakers
with their over-the-shoulder sleeknesses,
while being blindsided by mayoral candidates,
some of color, vying to meld neighborhoods.)
We can all get there together, can't we?
Some speak of "deliverables." Or "accountability."
(Why do they all speak Latinate derivatives?)
Do I have answers? I do not. Which is not
any reason to succumb to what you're now
feeling. For one, we can easily Google-
locate the French *fabricant* of the monthly
capsule that sterilizes the little suckers.
Second, I have pager numbers for a host
of men who fix broken shut-offs, cut T-joints
and apply plumber's dope shamelessly.
And once I get home I'll be working at
editing and journalizing our newsletter
to help embed corrective economizing
metrics at appropriate interstices. ...

Let us not in passing, my friends, become
the BLIND PEDS signs make us want to see.
I'm here to invite your outward-looking
suggestions and to solicit contributions
toward new PSAs (as long as they eschew
advocacy). It's not about me, you see.
But it's not about you either. Community
is what we're talking about. It's about
about. About how many of you are still
here, sitting on this floor, nodding gingerly,
"doing outreach" shoulder to shoulder.
Well, there you are! That's what it means
to reconfirm ourselves in the search for
common interests from occulted mutualities.
Yes, that's it—the meaty business that lies
just out of touch from resolution: rhetoric.

4

Musician. Comedian. Muralist

"The mind of man is fashioned and built up
even as a strain of music is."
—Wordsworth, 1799 *Prelude*

1. The Vocal Line

The voice alone cannot reproduce everything or
produce every effect; together, though, with the
expression of the whole the finer details of the poem
emerge, and all is well so long as the vocal line is not
sacrificed.
—Robert Schumann

Full of ham and eggs and cinnamon toast
and juice, and, just like that, he enters
his breakfast stage. Bran flakes in their
blue bowl get down to business. The plumbing
creaks, he can't say where. A hint of snow
goes by, that way it goes. Still, in the end
a good night. Then another. Then, morning.

And when geraniums on the window-sill
begin to flower, it fostered an aromatic
middle period. The pipe wrench found its socket.
Seating himself at the upright, hands in pockets,
trees at the window scripted a vocal line,
their liederkreis—but is that all they offered?

He dreams his wife climbs out of her side
to announce she is his lover. Climbing in,
the dog assures him she is hungry but still happy.
Pipes knock pianissimo. On the back burner: coffee's
sizzling coloratura. There's no main breaking.
He loves this house, its hemidemisemiquavers.

2. The Stand-Up's Constitutional

> *Fantastic brain. No ear.*
>> Pierre Boulez (composer/musical conductor)
>> on Iannis Xenakis (composer/engineer)

> *A fool lifteth up his voice with laughter,*
> *but a wise man doth scarce a little smile*
> Ecclesiasticus 21:20

Not bad, eh? he winked
rocking back, stock-still.
Then, sternly at me:. *See?*
No joke ever admits
how smart it is.

On we walked,
cigar ash flouring
the length of his overalls,
a handlebar mustache
licking at his collar.

A good laugh can be
Clocked. Out there. In
here, timing is content.
You watch. You listen.
(You call that listening?)

At the curve in the path
where the river
retrieves itself:
the town's oldest graveyard:
It's where they get

their names for streets.
Where he pointed,
is where I looked.
A boat rowed past.
You call that looking?

He had wrung his
handkerchief out.
What do you call this?
The air unfolded,
dripping with birds.

3. Across a Crowded Room

Through many long years I sang my songs.
But when I wanted to sing of joy
it turned to sorrow,
and when I wanted to sing of sorrow
it was transmuted into joy.

Thus was I divided between joy and sorrow.
                    —"The Diary of Franz Schubert" (1822)

When the wheel-lock of the antique
wood-stocked revolver went off
half-cocked in the next room, I
had just finished smoking the hand-
rolled cigarette you were probably
saving for the Colonel. There I stood
exhaling, yes, but inhaling also,
smarting a bit, the way a nicked
lip does before it goes bloody,
picturing how my hands might be
cupped where your braids shook
over your breasts like campaign ribbons.
But already I was forgetting,
you know, everything—
the life I'd give my life to hold
and the life I held in earnest.

In one room, on every wall,
hung tapestries, ancestors woven
into a few. In another room
dogs, each making its unique sound.
Back you came, blushing, dressed
as always to kill, into a world
filling fast with crowded rooms,
when something was uttered
or at least overhead, something
like: "Do you see any bodies?"
I didn't move. There was only mine.

And so today—say, it's raw
and spitting rain, as often of late,
I see how bruised your arms are,
like the feelings of younger sons,
or how your words still escape me
like people having run for their lives.

5

Fences: An Explanation

The Tohono O'odham Nation's ancestral home
in the Sonoran Desert is an area now part of both
the U.S. and Mexico. These "desert people,"
as they call themselves, practice flash-flood
farming, for they have no wells for water, nor
any word for 'walls.'

*

Water / will outwit / a wall
                   —Linda Gregerson, "Waterborne"

For me, growing up, the prairie began
on the west side of Berlin, a town in rural
Wisconsin, where I heard Spanish, a language
not taught here, more often in the streets
than English. If a prairie is to language
what hearing is to speaking, could prairies be
where analogies are grounded? What,
back then, I felt, between the words I heard
and those I spoke was a fence, a property line.

Other fences, it seemed, were meant to check
the prairie's dream of reaching infinitude,
to give wilderness corners, to make it yield
fields. But "fields," I learned, changed seasonally.
At harvest, some fields ineluctably
became impromptu camps housing those
whose labor culled the planted ones and whose
words arose in the streets but not in any schools.

More fences were also arising, vanishing,
one of crosshatched wood, open at the base,
not fixed to frame any fields but in season to
stop snow blowing off their stubble onto roads.

Many years later, I visited that other
Berlin, whose Wall, preceding my arrival,
had marked the divide between the victors once
allied, now leaving only reptilian footprints
like those my host showed us near his front lawn.

Elsewhere, however, the Wall had been restored—
notably at Checkpoint Charlie—to please
people with cameras (one German translation for
"tourists") who view history as f-stops.
Walls, though, mostly originate in fear
grown contagious—cf. Hadrian's migratory
forces, whose wall now monumentalizes
itself alone. Even if you can see over it or
through it, like the chain-link encircling Stonehenge,
a wall is a thrill, analogous to Power.

But if Walden, the name of Thoreau's own adopted
backyard, seemed to mean "walled in," as if
to wall out Concord, that was to misread
Thoreau's emerging resistance to fences, his
sense of a new perspective. In his
lexicon, "in" and "out" were verbal hinges—

in effect, to a wall, what a light is to a stage
scrim, a hung fabric which becomes opaque
or invisible depending on how
that light is placed, whether in front or behind it.
In respect to light, a wall is what marks us,
bestowing an identity upon us—out or in.
But the wall or fence is itself, then, only
where our perspectival senses culminate.
Call it a vanishing point.

        Or so, almost
a century later after Thoreau, the First Lady
acted it out—well, almost—when she stood
at the vanishing point of the sea, where the U.S.
had fenced the Tijuana estuary. Watching
the Pacific lap at the border of her America
she celebrated it with winged words,
"I hope this fence won't be here much longer,"
then crossed the barbed wire to the festive side,
the park named Friendship, the music mariachi.

    (But the erased vanishing point:
    did it unfence both sides' identity
    or only restore each side's identity?)

———

Water: in the tongue of the self-named "desert people"
not to have a word for water needs no bordering
(no wells, no walls). Nameless, too, is water,
it seems, for those who see, as Emily says,
New Englandly. In Frost's odd poem what upends
a wall is a mere "something"—not named as water's
climate-specific capacity to freeze and thaw.

The analogy for this fencing, this linkage
of land and water, is the way some believe
that hearing others speak their own language
means they want to speak it back to them,
to find ears that can float words walls cannot outwit,
as in the famous saga of the out-sized catfish
landed off one bank and the off-color one
off the other—events that sadden the outside
world as toxic proof of general global mischief—
but those living on different sides of the river
eat whichever fish they catch, whatever
name it has for them, however they
self-identify, until the hot wind, dying,
hymns its one refrain: *Even when dry, all rivers*
run deep. That's why, in time, they try crossing
the river bottoms, the hardening fish-scale mud,
their slow steps wandering, still a little wet,
singing the fall of each fence still facing them.

Ground Cover in Flyover Country

Racial issues? All any of us could
remember was none. Until one of us
remembered one black face one time
in a high school assembly. No Orientals,
though, so soon after the big wars.
though there was a "chop suey" house
in town where a few of us remembered
eating, thinking, back then, how good
it was, how "different," though un-
certain we'd feel so going back now.
Still, we'd heard the place was still
"holding on." This put another one
of us in mind of a friend, an "islander"
(Caribbean probably some adult said),
whose last name we mis-heard as "Marcus."

The Klan tried once to hold a rally
here, but we protested and the Rotarians
talked the City Council out of it.
At a White Sox game, some years later,
one reminded the rest of us what a few
by then knew—that there were three
Black families by our senior year and
there were never three but always four
Jewish ones, "for those of you who really
want to know." Because I did, I stood
corrected, thinking myself anew less a
a product of "issues" than my family's
"concerns," were I to marry a Catholic
girl, "when I grew up." No one worried
I might be gay. Should they have?

Precedents

It's not tradition that matters;
it's precedents.
                    —Hugh MacDiarmid

Another month. And again no obits
inside its covers, no excerpts from
deceased contributors. Good news,
that, in the poetry world. Only now,
ten years after his death, just a few
poems by Edwin Morgan published
for the first time inside the *pages*
of this prestigious journal founded
eight years before he was born.

"I, Morgan," he would write, "whom the Romans called
Pelagius." (Readers of *Poetry*: look it up.)

This one, this Morgan
(whom intimates called Eddie), I met
once, thanks to JC, at his poetry reading
in Edinburgh, a town built like his own
Glasgow, his "green Cathures" on a "frisky
firth of salmon," and we, a version of
what other Celtic folk, the neighboring Welsh,
call *cymry* (comrades) after their self-
named nation (Cymru) set forth, of course,
afterwards, for whisky. He was elderly
even then, of gentle mien, and gracious
to a very young American with even

fewer than a handful of poems
to show for himself.
    Nor had I yet
discovered *him*. How he had made even
pedestrian lines of Shakespeare's—

  Lady Macbeth: What is your tidings?
  Messenger: The King comes here tonight.
  Lady Macbeth: Thou'rt mad to say it!

speak the impending threat in Scots—

  Leddy Macbeth: Ye bring me news?
  Castle Carle: This nicht ye hae a guest—the king.
  Leddy Macbeth: Are ye wud?

———————

Morgan would live another quarter-century
from the evening we drank to our mutual health.
His *Complete Poems* would not be published
until the year of his death, the year that I was,
thanks to GM, supposed to meet
Hugh MacDiarmid (intimates called him
Chris) at his cottage outside the city.
The press that would eventually publish
my first book had recently been his first
American publisher, and so I had read

The Drunk Man the year before my year
abroad in Scotland, but I had not yet
discovered "On A Raised Beach," either
the poem's own verbal lithogenesis or
the storm-strewn thing itself. Someone,
though, told me how MacDiarmid told
the difference, solely by their sound,
between the three rivers near his birthplace.
I knew once how a river named Rock
sounded to my teenaged ear nothing
like what its name augured, and later,
how the Derwent, or so Wordsworth
claimed, flowed through his dreams.
But three rivers? In rural Scotland? An
ear so fine? All I could picture was
Pittsburgh, its three for me for so long
largely unpronounceable ones.

———————

Thanks to the many friends who tried,
I nearly learned how to pronounce
Rhossili, Langharne, Tawe, Llanelli,
but once away from Wales I could
reliably hit only a few. Dear Gwyneth,
though, explained how, in a word
like Caerphilly, for example, the double
vowel between the /c/ and /r/

is rather more aspirated than articulated,
the mouthy delights of Welsh. Dai
it was, of course, eminent historian,
told how a few intimates, his father
foremost among them, dared call his
only begotten son "Dullin," the Welsh
pronunciation, and, Dai added, "Because
you know—having already dined with—
Aeronwy, and because you are a poet
and call yourself a teacher, you need
to know."

———————————

Know? I am the age my father
was when I moved here. Did he seem
that old back then? Do I? This year
he would be 115. He preferred to
sign his own name with his initials
F and W like T.S. or W.B. and always
capitalized that lonesome Z
splitting his last name into two
proper nouns. (Intimates called him
"Heinie," what some, perhaps not
intimates, also called Lou Gehrig,
also a German speaker, although my
father's archaic torso, his Popeye-
forearms fit a farmer, not a slugger.)

On the backs of old photos, Dad's
slightly flowery neat small hand:

Großmutter

Boy that thing could go

Eddie and Barb
upstairs tenants

The first hard-topped road
in the county

The boys (6 and 3)

John H. Kundert 1874-1932

> (My grandfather. "You
> once called him 'Black
> Jack.' Why?" "He could
> be hard to please.")

And on the back of another:

Kathryn Wichser

> (My grandmother. She died
> when I was 7 and spoke only

German, even when reading
to us boys English books.)

———————

And then one day a few months ago
my mother and father resurfaced,
seated together at what must have been
in its day a fashionable "supper club,"
judging by the souvenir cover

Nino Milo's Mocambo
"Powell at Bay"   San Francisco

and facing their smiling photo
what must have been his shipmates
from the Howell Lykes's quarter-
mastering, island-hopping, mopping-
up mission in the South Pacific.

Each had inscribed his name
and his address back home

Johnny Leamon, Lancaster, PA

Will Miller, New Orleans

Jackie Posados, White Plains, New York

Like all good immigrants my father
had enlisted after Pearl, as perhaps
they had, but he was a decade older,
perhaps might never have been drafted,
born when one Roosevelt, Teddy,
was President to fight a war in the name
of another Roosevelt, a relative of my
not-yet-wife. Assigned to boot camp
a few miles from where I would eventually
live over forty years in Texas, he would end
at sea, fighting, one assumes, on purpose,
people whose names were not like his.
These four were not to be members
of every reunion class. Only my father would
live out virtually the whole 20th century.

———————

And now, in my hand the hand
of my father, on the inside
of the menu's back cover:

4-11-45

(their wedding anniversary—
at that time having seen each other
only three times in three years)

At that time he was nearly 40,
the age I, his first child, would be
when my first child was born
and I would be attending college
exactly 20 years after that photo,
my freshman roommate from
White Plains, and I would write
often, later, about a poet born
a few days earlier in April but
175 years before. …

———————

Before? But so many
"afters" and "befores,"
so many histories you
toss tow-lines between.

And then that purple wave
spelling out its "after all"—

a text you may wish to skip
"lest," an Anglicism my
father surely never used,
you end up resigned

the rest of your life
to thinking your own
life a subject only you
remain the intimate of.

Notes

Condos in Cornfields. The French epigraph is *"la lune trop haute, / qui vaporise les bois."*

Ode to a Toaster. The form of this poem imitates that of Pablo Neruda's *Elemental Odes.*

Where Do You Come From? The title quotes from Pablo Neruda's *No Hay Olvido (Sonata).* Blaise Cendrars (born Frédéric Louis Sauser in La Chaux-de-Fonds, Switzerland) purports to take a train ride from Paris to Siberia in his magnificent 2-meter-tall accordion book, created with Sonia Delaunay, called *Prose du Transsibérien et de la Petite Jeanne de France* ("Prose of the Trans-Siberian and of the Little Jeanne of France").

First Assignment. This is the complete and unedited text of a three-paragraph essay written by a ninth-grade student.

Pedagogy. The Raj steadfastly refused to believe that tea grew or could grow in India, preferring to imagine tea as Chinese, coffee as Indian.

Post-Conquest. The poem textualizes an actual outdoor space near where a work by Gonzalo Fonseca, a Uruguayan artist, part of the School of the South (the Taller Torres-Garcia) was exhibited. This work, "Graneros III," is sculpted from a smallish block of red travertine marble to resemble a combination of granary and Mesoamerican temple, with indentations that look like kivas, external steps to altarlike platforms, and assorted free-standing shapes, some resembling eggs, one clearly a foot, like those in Mayan hieroglyphs.

Le Tombeau de Paul Celan. Paul Celan, the pen name for the Romanian-born, German-language poet Paul Ancel, lived in Paris after World War II. Pont Mirabeau is where Avenue Emile Zola meets the River Seine. The Marquis and Compte de Mirabeau lived in the French Revolutionary period; Zola is from the Dreyfus period a century later. Guillaume Apollinaire, born Wilhelm-Apollinaris de Kostrowitzky, was of eastern Europe ancestry like Celan and assumed his *nom de plume*, like Celan, after taking up residence in Paris; he also wrote a poem called "Le Pont Mirabeau." Celan's actual grave is located some miles from Paris. "No one / witnesses for the / witness" is a quotation from one of his poems. My poem also alludes to Celan's unique way of compounding nouns. The "tombeau" of the title alludes to a poetic series of *hommages* by Stéphane Mallarmé. I am grateful to John Felstiner's monumental study of Celan for some narrative details.

Bifocals. Peterson's refers to the popular bird guides written by Roger Tory Peterson.

Ground Wars. For Albert Goldbarth

Like Hershey's for Chocolate. "Today" in the poem is the

winter of 2001, marking the start of the American assault in Afghanistan.

Visiting the Somme. The setting of the poem is the World War I battlefield and environs. *Rhyme* is a late addition to English orthography, replacing *rime*, for reasons suggested in the poem. The classicist W. R. Johnson in *The Idea of Lyric* translates "rhythm" as "zigazggedness." Siegfried Sassoon survived the war; Wilfred Owen did not. Two French phrases are not translated in the poem itself: *les arbres d'alignement*, the trees planted to line the sides of roads; and *de bon marché*, "priced attractively."

Allianoi. The poem refers to this precious archaeological site in Turkey, one featuring ancient baths, which, at the time of my visit, were all threatened with destruction by the damming of a nearby river to create a lake to facilitate irrigation practices. The dam was eventually built in 2010 over massive protests, and the spa, dating from the early Roman empire, was flooded and lost.

The poem is dedicated to Cliff and the late Selhan Endres.

What We Thought We Came For. When Xanthos, the capital of ancient Lycia, was attacked by the Persians, the men of Xanthos, rather than surrender, tried to commit mass suicide by first burning their women and children. Enough survived that the city remained viable. Centuries later, when besieged by Brutus during the Roman civil war, the citizens of Xanthos once again resorted to mass suicide rather than capitulate. Only 150 survived.

The Devil's Rosary. The above-ground rock formation alluded to here, *le chapelet du diable*, is near the more famous caves of the Dordogne region, especially the one at Villars. Ligneras, a hamlet of some seven houses or so, just a short walk from St. Estèphe, is rarely marked on maps; nor is there any road sign to it. This is the region whose Roman name Ezra Pound revived: *provincia deserta*. The poem is dedicated to my hosts there, Marie-Claude Perrin and her family.

North of Austin: 1980. For Janis Bergman Carton

Way Out West. This is the title of a ground-breaking LP from the late 1950s by the Sonny Rollins Trio in which Western standards, such as "I'm an Old Cowhand," are given jazz treatments.

Another's Brass. Some narrative details in the poem are derived from Robert D. Richardson, Jr., *Henry Thoreau: A Life of the Mind*, University of California Press, 1986. The poem alludes to *A Week on the Concord and Merrimack Rivers* in which Thoreau uses such words as "tantivy" and "pellicular." A "swallet" is an underground hole in limestone that permits water to enter or drain.

Ronsard's Complaint. I offer this version in tribute to W.B. Yeats, whose own version marks him as one of the masters at "writing with others."

The Sun. I offer this version in tribute to Donald Wesling, who made a brilliant example of this Baudelaire poem ("Le Soleil") in his book *The Chances of Rhyme* and to Charles Tomlinson for his poem "The Chances of Rhyme."

To Rimbaud. For Lucia Woodruff

Post-Op. i.m. Michael Adams

Ode: Pandemic/Invasion. Emmanuel Macron, President of France, remarked, well after the Russian invasion of Crimea and then Ukraine, that this was a further manifestation of the global Covid pandemic.

Fences: An Explanation. The "First Lady" is Mrs. Pat Nixon at the dedication on the border with Tijuana.

About

A native of Wisconsin, Kurt Heinzelman attended school in New England; held a Fulbright at Edinburgh University (Scotland); was awarded a Rockefeller Grant to Bellagio (Italy); and lived for many years in Austin where he taught Poetry and Poetics as well as British Romanticism at the University of Texas where he is now Professor Emeritus. Elected to the Texas Institute of Letters, he was also appointed an Honorary Professor at Swansea University (Wales) for his service on behalf of the International Dylan Thomas Prize. An editor, literary historian, and translator, his sixth collection of poems is *Pollen, Salt, & Chimes*. He and his wife, the scholar Susan Sage Heinzelman, live in Southern California.

Responses to Previous Works

"Heinzelman's ... collection [*Intimacies & Other Devices*] is ... replete both with intimacies and with the great range of devices poets and lovers employ. ...[T]hese poems are wildly imaginative and very, very sexy."

—Ellen Doré Watson, poet, editor, and translator of Brazilian poetry and fiction

"It is wonderful to experience a poet's bounty ..., to participate in the playful re-interpretation of long traditions in the hands of one who knows, to feel the spring of poetic rhythm and the eloquence of the intricately concentrated expression, as memory, desire, humor and sensuality are shaped in virtuosic language."

—Nicholas Jose, novelist and editor of *The Literature of Australia* (Norton)

"I must say how much I love these poems for their delightfully fresh expression one finds on page after page, as if a dozen ventriloquists in a painting by, say, René Magritte were addressing you. So many surprises here with poetic forms and topics. How aptly named this collection is: *Whatever You May Say*. Four words which Heinzelman approaches with half a century of wit and savvy philosophical inquiry behind him, and all presented lightly with such sprezzatura."

—Paul Mariani, poet, scholar, and author of critical biographies of William Carlos Williams, Wallace Stevens, Hart Crane, and others.

"Rich and inventive, Kurt Heinzelman's poems are funny, serious, and everything in between, often all at once … These poems are sometimes boisterous and sometimes sad, sometimes learned and sometimes comic, but always a pleasure."

—Lawrence Raab, National Book Award Finalist for *Mistaking Each Other for Ghosts*

"I was thoroughly prepared to enjoy this new book and I was not disappointed. Heinzelman's poems consistently possess the qualities of music and intelligence without which poetry cannot be good."

—Steven Weinberg, Nobel Laureate in Physics, author of *To Explain the World*

"Kurt Heinzelman's newest collection is filled with lines 'drawn taut as water plaiting down.' Strikingly vivid and often hilarious and wise, the poems here meditate on a wide range of subjects, from the history of sunflowers, barking dogs, the Texas landscape(s), postures and behaviors of dachshunds, the vagaries of memory, to wars of all sorts and in various parts of the world. If only for the luscious sounds of the 'chittering flocks of swallows [that] prey / At evening on the antiquities of the day'; for the witty list in 'Songbirds of Oz'; for the dynamite line 'eggy slidings of slapstick blue' that ends 'Skyscrapers by the Sea'; and for the surprising ending of 'North of Austin': 'where turkey buzzards rotate / slowly overhead like couples / all aglitter underneath their / honkytonk's mirrored ball,' and for much more, Heinzelman's *Whatever You May Say* is not a book to miss!

—Wendy Barker, winner of the John Ciardi Poetry Prize for One Blackbird at a Time. Her last collection was *Weave: New and Selected Poems*

"In *The Names They Found There* Heinzelman creates a poetry of place with an unerring eye and ear for the ways that landscape can be mapped in the twists and turns of language. As in his previous wonderful book, The Halfway Tree, he displays, in equal parts, a mastery of sight, sound, and intellection."

—Michael Davidson, author of many critical studies including *Ghostlier Demarcations: Modern Poetry and the Material Word*, he is also one the pioneering scholars in Disability Studies

"*The Names They Found There* travels from Pflugerville to Wellfleet, Australia to Istanbul. Its poems, populated by Ben Franklin and Jacobus Vrel, Sonny Rollins and Warren Spahn, speak of flying foxes and fricatives, baseball and pêches jaunes, sweet corn and Incan quipus and 'capless Bics in a Styrofoam cup' at a taco kiosk on concrete blocks. 'And what of all this / luminous / curiosity,' one of Heinzelman's poems asks. ... [T]he question can be answered in musical terms: Heinzelman's curiosity is luminous, yes, but also canorous, 'A continuo of / the familiar, ... under which / discontinuities / of the exotic.'"

—H. L. Hix, author of many books including *Chromatic* (Finalist for the National Book Award) and *As Easy as Lying: Essays on Poetry*

"These poems artfully negotiate what we know by name and what we know by heart. These poems travel; each 'road spills / its cargo of hooks.' What a thrill to discover this etymology of place, of self."

—Susan B. A. Somers-Willett, besides her award-winning poetry collections and her ground-breaking critical work *The Cultural Politics of Slam Poetry*, she has been celebrated for her multi-genre study of women living below the poverty line in upstate New York: *Women of Troy*

"Heinzelman commands 'any stroke of available light' to deliver luminous concoctions of history, music, and heart. A beautiful smart book."

—Barbara Ras, editor of Trinity University Press and author of *Bite Every Sorrow* (Walt Whitman Award from the Academy of American Poets) and most recently *The Blues of Heaven*

"At a time when so many poets whittle themselves down into defining personal styles and subjects—into what the Polish poet Adam Zagajewski has dubbed 'deft miniaturists of a single theme'—Kurt Heinzelman writes a restless, free-ranging poetry, rarely repeating a form or approach. In a Heinzelman book, you're likely to encounter ballads, Pindaric odes, sonnets, ekphrastic poems, short lyrics, one-sentence poems, and long, elastic sequences, all handled with remarkable skill and ease."

—Brian Barker, author of *The Black Ocean* and *Vanishing Acts* (both Crab Orchard Poetry Awards)

"*Whatever You May Say* immerses us in the contemplative poetics of Kurt Heinzelman, weaving between humor and essence and wit, touching our need to understand this chaotic world around us, with a steady philosophy of spirit and light: "Where to enter is to go all the way in."

—karla k. morton, 2010 Texas Poet Laureate, author of *Accidental Origami, New and Selected Poems*

"*Intimacies & Other Devices* [is] a wonderful book, one that will bring pleasure, in the deepest sense, to all who encounter it."

—Michael Blumenthal, prize-winning poet, educator, lawyer, and translator from the Hungarian

Milton Keynes UK
Ingram Content Group UK Ltd.
UKHW031154061224
452240UK00001B/174